Persuasive Business Presentations

Persuasive Business Presentations

Using the Problem-Solution Method to Influence Decision Makers to Take Action

Gary L. May

First published in 2014 by
Business Expert Press, LLC
222 East 46th Street, New York, NY 10017
www.businessexpertpress.com

ISBN-13: 978-1-60649-468-4 (paperback)
ISBN-13: 978-1-60649-469-1 (e-book)

Business Expert Press Corporate Communication Collection

Collection ISSN: 2156-8162 (print)
Collection ISSN: 2156-8170 (electronic)

Cover and interior design by Exeter Premedia Services Private Ltd., Chennai, India

First edition: 2014

10 9 8 7 6 5 4 3 2 1

Printed in the United States of America.

Abstract

Business life is about persuasion. Effective managers advance their careers by identifying problems, developing solutions, and persuading decision makers to provide the support and resources necessary to make things happen. This book focuses on a specific presentation context: a problem–solution persuasive presentation to decision makers delivered in a conference room environment. Such presentations occur at every level in an organization. Therefore, team leaders, supervisors, managers, and executives can all benefit from learning how to design and deliver powerful presentations that move decision makers to take action. The author blends his extensive business experience with current research on persuasion to provide a practical, applied approach to using the problem–solution pattern. An integrated case study provides examples for each step in the process. The result is a useful, actionable guide that will help professionals from every field make a difference in their organization.

Keywords

persuasion, presentation, problem–solution pattern.

Contents

Introduction

I vividly remember the first time I participated in a truly persuasive business presentation.

I grew up working in my family's wholesale distribution business. My father founded the business in the basement of our house, and the company grew to be a large, very successful regional operation. After graduating from college, I joined my father full time, and we worked together for 17 years. His charge to me was "bring us into the next generation."

At one point, I had responsibility for sales, purchasing, and data processing and was working on improving our purchasing systems. We had recently upgraded our computer system to the IBM 360 series, and I wanted to move to an online, interactive purchasing process. IBM had a relatively new purchasing software program for the 360 called INVEN-3. I asked our IBM representative to study our needs and make a presentation to my father, the purchasing team, and me. The package was quite expensive, and I knew there would be a lot of resistance, not only because of the cost, but also because it would force us to change many of our procedures.

The approach by the IBM representative and her manager was fascinating. They defined our problems by comparing our performance data, such as inventory turn rate and out-of-stock percentage, to industry benchmarks. We were below par. They translated the differences into financial terms by showing, for example, the savings in inventory carrying costs we could achieve by increasing our inventory turns. As they worked through the numbers, they obtained agreement on each underlying assumption. My dad, as the crafty entrepreneur he was, insisted that they reduce their projected savings by at least half on each component.

The IBM representative also shared success stories from other companies in the wholesale trade, including two respected noncompetitor companies in our trade association. We learned that we would be the first in our class of trade in the southeast to implement the package and that IBM would work to make us a "showcase" installation.

The IBMers also had a third person on their team that day: Anders Herlitz, the inventor of INVEN-3 and the leader of the development team. Anders was very impressive—an older gentleman, Swedish born with a lovely accent. He was brilliant and engaging in answering the technical questions from the buying staff.

In the conclusion, when the IBM representative pulled all the economic assumptions and potential savings that we had agreed to into a final number and compared it to the cost of installation and fees, the annual savings was significantly greater than the cost. That made my dad happy, especially as he had insisted that they cut the projected savings in half. The buyers were excited because the new system would be easier to use compared to our current stock-card system and could address most of their technical concerns. I was pleased because the move to a new system would help fulfill my father's charge to me to be an innovator in our region. The IBM team persuaded us that day to make the decision to move forward.

When I returned to my office, I closed my door and meditated on what I had just experienced. I had a profound sense that the presentation I had participated in, the structure and approach, offered great potential for me personally, as a leader and manager, and for our company, in terms of business development. I resolved to learn all I could about the process of persuasion and effective presentations and began a lifelong exploration of the principles.

Most fundamental principles are old and characterized by their simplicity. I discovered that the Ancient Greeks codified the three key elements of persuasive appeal. Aristotle called the elements *logos* (logic), *pathos* (emotion), and *ethos* (character and credibility). He taught that effective persuasion must incorporate all three elements. Most of the literature on persuasion today draws from Aristotle's work. Figure I.1 provides a model of the elements of persuasion in what I call the "Persuasion Triangle."[1]

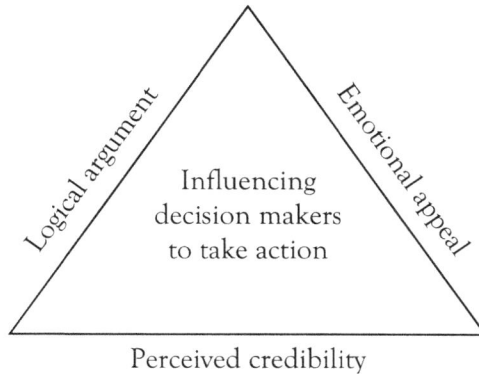

Logical argument

Emotional appeal

Influencing
decision makers
to take action

Perceived credibility

Figure I.1. The persuasion triangle.

Think about the model in terms of the story I just told you.

How did the IBMers use logic? They supported their position with facts and data. It is important to see that they interpreted the *meaning* of the data. To say that the software could help us achieve a 95% service level (in-stock condition) is not very meaningful. To say that our current service level was 92% and then show the impact of the additional percentage points on increasing sales and reducing operating costs—that is meaningful. Numbers and facts by themselves are not persuasive. You have to relate the numbers to some benchmark, such as past performance, industry averages, or goals, and draw some conclusions from the data.

Note also that logic requires organization to make it easy to follow. The IBMers used a problem–solution pattern. They defined and documented the problem (e.g., lost sales from out of stocks), presented the solution (INVEN-3 forecasting system), showed the benefits (improved sales, lower costs), addressed concerns, and asked for agreement. The IBMers built their case systematically, linking a series of problem—solution cycles.

How did the IBMers use emotional appeal? They shared success stories of other distributors, applying a psychological principle from behavioral science called *social proof*.[2] We are always interested in what our peers are doing—people tend to follow the lead of others who are similar. We also were intrigued about becoming a "showcase" for our region. That appealed to our pride; we all value recognition.

Finally, how did the IBMers employ credibility? They had Anders Herlitz there—the author of the program. Anders exuded credibility—appearance, expertise, and personality. In addition, for your audience to view you as credible, you have to demonstrate that you have done your homework, for example, citing trustworthy sources for your information (the IBM representative collected data from our buyers and from the National Association of Wholesale Distributors).

Credibility also depends on the relationships you have developed with your audience. You have to demonstrate that you have put yourself in their shoes and care about their concerns and issues. Our IBM representative had served us well and built a level of trust. We believed she had our best interests at heart.

As Aristotle taught, persuasion requires the integrated use of all three elements of the Persuasion Triangle. In addition, the structure and delivery of the presentation play an important role in your ability to influence decision makers to take action. You want your messages to be audience centered, logically arranged, and packaged to facilitate easy understanding and action. The secret is to use the appropriate pattern for the type of communication situation and message.

Different purposes, such as informational, instructional, good news, bad news, and persuasive presentations, require different organizing patterns. Using a pattern, proven by research and practice, saves time and produces a better product. If you are expecting resistance to your persuasive message, the best pattern to use is the *problem–solution* method, the focus of this book. You can apply and adapt the problem–solution pattern to a number of business situations, including sales and business development.

Figure I.2 diagrams the flow of the problem–solution structure and serves as an outline for Part I of our discussion, developing a problem–solution presentation.

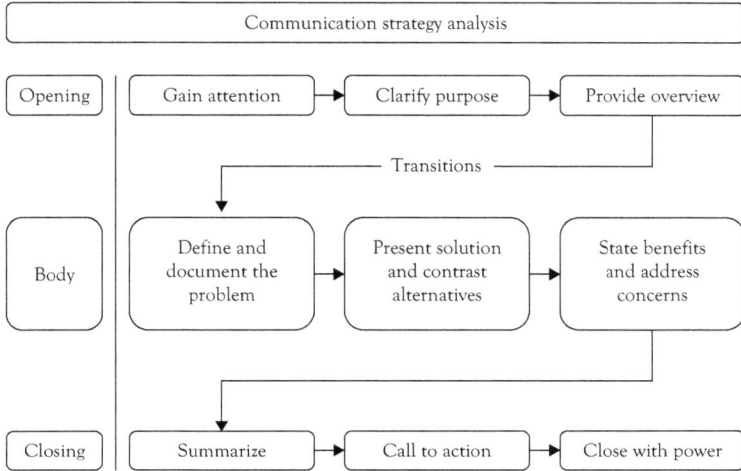

Figure I.2. Problem–solution presentation pattern.

Part II of the book addresses issues related to presentation delivery, including designing visuals, rehearsing, presenting in an engaging manner, and handling questions. I will be assuming a conference room environment, the most typical venue for problem–solution presentations to decision makers.

An integrated case study will supply examples for each step in the process. Figure I.3 provides the background on the case. Please read the case before proceeding to Chapter 1, where we will begin our exploration of the problem–solution model by learning how to conduct a communication strategy analysis.

My purpose for this book is to blend my years of business experience with current research on persuasion to provide a practical, applied approach to using the principles of the Persuasion Triangle and the problem–solution pattern in a conference room setting. Along the way, I will also include some tips from presentation experts that have been particularly meaningful to me. My goal is to produce a useful, actionable guide that will help you, as a business professional, make a difference in your organization and advance your career.

Thank you for investing your time and joining me in this learning experience.

Making a Case for a Tuition Reimbursement Plan

You are Carson Rodrequez, the Human Resources Regional Vice President (VP) for Serv-Pro, Inc., a Chicago-based specialty foods distribution and service firm. Your region provides specialty food products and retail support services to supermarkets throughout the southeast through a network of five distribution centers.

Specialty, ethnic, and natural foods are growing category segments in supermarkets. Your region is expanding very fast to accommodate the demand and is experiencing significant staffing and employee retention problems, especially among salaried and professional employees. Currently, the region is losing 20% of its 325 salaried employees a year, which is above the industry norm of 12%. The statistics are similar in other regions. In addition, margins are under pressure from some larger competitors (the result of recent mergers) who are using their economies of scale to cut prices to gain market share. The company is also making the transition from being a traditional wholesaler to a more sophisticated supply chain/logistics firm that is able to provide a variety of distribution services, technology support, and retail-level category management and merchandising services for retail customers.

As a new Regional VP of Human Resources, you believe Serv-Pro needs to improve the benefits package for Serv-Pro employees, both to help attract new employees and reduce turnover. One benefit you would like the company to consider is a college tuition reimbursement plan (TRP). As the business environment becomes more sophisticated, the company needs to upgrade current staff through training and additional education. A TRP would demonstrate the company's commitment to retooling its work force. In addition, most of your major competitors offer a TRP.

Given the financial environment, you expect resistance to the idea of tuition reimbursement from some members of the corporate benefits committee. The committee consists of corporate executives from various operating functions. Susan Rhome, the Senior VP of Human Resources and your boss, is on the committee. The current chair is the Executive VP of Finance.

You have talked with Susan about the TRP idea and, while skeptical, she agreed to talk with the benefits committee chair and arrange for a one-hour time slot on the benefits committee agenda. You have 30 days to conduct the necessary research and develop a presentation on the feasibility of implementing a TRP. Susan directed you to determine what similar companies are doing with TRPs and examine the potential costs, benefits, and pitfalls for Serv-Pro.

Figure I.3. Case situation: Serv-Pro tuition reimbursement plan.

PART I
Developing a Problem-Solution Presentation

CHAPTER 1

Conducting a Communication Strategy Analysis

Happily experimenting with the problem–solution method to help develop business for our family wholesale distribution company, I was in the conference room of a regional supermarket chain making a presentation on the financial benefits of our services for selected product categories. The target audience, in my mind, was the Vice President (VP) of Purchasing, who, at my request, had invited his staff to participate in the presentation and discussion. But the Purchasing VP had also invited a manager from the accounting department. The accounting manager aggressively challenged some of the assumptions in my financial models as they applied to her organization and pretty well wrecked the presentation, embarrassing me in the process. I learned later that the power in the organization resided in the accounting function, and the purchasing department rarely made vendor decisions without this particular accounting manager's involvement. I had failed to do my homework about my audience and how the decision-making process worked in this particular organization.

I learned my lesson the hard way. The first step in developing an effective problem–solution presentation is to slow down and think through some questions to help focus your persuasive strategy and tactics. Over the years, I've refined a series of questions designed for the problem–solution persuasive pattern. These questions "prime the pump" for thinking about how to strategically approach the presentation. Brainstorming and "white boarding" the answers with your team are always the first steps in presentation development.[1] Here are the eight primary questions for analysis:

1. What is the problem you are trying to solve?
2. What is the purpose or outcome you want to achieve?
3. What is your central message?

4. Who is your target audience and how do they make decisions?

5. What are the contextual factors that may influence your message?

6. What information do you need to include to build support for your position?

7. What are the benefits to your audience?

8. What potential objections will you need to address or minimize?

Although the questions may appear linear in nature, developing a communication strategy is really an iterative process. As you work through a question, you may need to revisit and edit your answers to a previous question. I will share some thoughts about each question in the following sections, using our case study (presented in the introduction) to provide example applications. As a reminder, in the case situation, Carson Rodrequez, the Regional VP of Human Resources for Serv-Pro, is preparing a presentation to the corporate benefits committee, advocating the implementation of a tuition reimbursement plan.

What Is the Problem?

You must be clear on the problem you are trying to solve and understand how the problem affects the organization or group. The problem has to be costing the organization something of value, such as time, inconvenienced customers, reduced productivity, or excessive waste. You must show how the problem ultimately impacts one of more of the key concerns of decision makers: financial performance, customer satisfaction, employee morale and productivity, or the company's strategic vision and mission. Business is about numbers, and you must seek to turn the problem into a dollars-and-cents issue.

In our case situation, the problem is excessive turnover of salaried employees. The region is losing 20% of its salaried employees per year, compared to the industry norm of 12%. Other regions are experiencing similar turnover rates. Turnover costs the company money and affects productivity. It is expensive to replace a knowledge worker, and Carson will need to quantify that cost.

In addition, losing knowledgeable employees makes it more difficult for the company to make the transition from being a traditional wholesaler to a more sophisticated supply chain/logistics firm. So, the issue also relates to the company's new vision and mission.

What Is Your Purpose?

You must be specific in your purpose statement. What do you want your audience to do as a result of your presentation? I recommend you write your purpose as a full declarative sentence.

Here, for example, is the preliminary draft of Carson's purpose statement based on our case study:

> *My purpose is to persuade the Benefits Committee to approve a 2-year pilot implementation of a Tuition Reimbursement Plan (TRP) in the southeast region beginning calendar year 2014.*

Note that the statement has a clear rhetorical purpose (to persuade), a specific target audience (members of the Benefits Committee), and a specific action (approval of a pilot TRP with an implementation date).

The use of the word "pilot" requires some explanation. My philosophy, when attempting to convince decision makers to approve a project that takes the company into uncharted territory, has some financial risk, or both, is to think incrementally. Carson has to make a strong case for the TRP, but he will have to make certain assumptions, based on research, which may be debatable, such as how many employees will use the benefit or how much the program can reduce turnover. By recommending a pilot or test in a limited area, Carson can lower the risk and position the project, in effect, as research, a test of a hypothesis that will generate some data specific for his organization. If he does a good job applying the elements of the Persuasion Triangle—logic, emotion, and credibility—most executives will be comfortable (and curious) enough to support the project so that they can see the outcome data. Such an approach also sets up the expectation of periodic progress reports, which means more "face time" with the committee, a career enhancer, assuming Carson manages the project well.

What Is Your Central Message?

The specific purpose of the presentation is what you hope to accomplish. The central message is the BIG IDEA you want people to remember. It is the answer to the question audience members often receive when they return to their office and coworkers ask "What was the takeaway from the meeting?"

Here is Carson's draft statement of his central message to the Benefits Committee:

> *A Tuition Reimbursement Plan can help reduce costs by improving employee retention, and it can help attract the type of employees we need to support our new strategy.*

As this example demonstrates, the central message statement captures the main themes Carson will develop in the body of his presentation. After Carson completes his research, he can refine the statement to crystallize his message further.

Presenting effectively is a matter of ruthless focus. As you know from your own experience, listening to a presentation is hard work, and people do not retain much of what they hear. Help your audience by being very clear about the BIG IDEA. Keep it simple. Keep it focused.

Who Is Your Target Audience?

The purpose statement identifies the target audience, but you need to dig below the surface and think about who is going to be in the conference room, in particular, the key decision makers and thought leaders. Effective presenters are audience-centered, connecting in meaningful ways with the audience's goals, values, and interests. Every person in the room arrives with two questions on their mind: Why is this important and how does this affect me? Carson has to answer those questions.

There are many ways to analyze the audience. Table 1.1 provides some examples that appear frequently in books and articles on presentation skills, all with cautions about stereotyping and overgeneralizing.[2]

These particular methods are useful when dealing with a small, relatively homogeneous group or when you are selling in a one-on-one

Table 1.1. Example Ways to Analyze an Audience

Method	Example factors	Why important
Demographics	Age, Gender, Education, Ethic/ Cultural Background, Religion, Group Membership (e.g., NRA vs. Sierra Club)	Adjust language and examples to appeal to different values and priorities; avoid biased or inflammatory language
Decision Style	Charismatic, Thinker, Skeptic, Follower, Controller	Adjust content and delivery to meet the preferred style for making decisions
Personality Type (e.g., Myers–Briggs)	Introvert vs. Extravert; Sensing vs. Intuitive; Thinking vs. Feeling; Perceiving vs. Judging	Adjust content and delivery to meet preferences and play to the strengths of each type
Learning Style	Auditory, Visual, Kinesthetic	Design delivery to appeal to the various learning style needs

situation. However, for most audiences, the demographics will be diverse, and the audience will represent multiple decision styles, personality types, and learning styles. So what can you do?

Based on my experience, given a business presentation context, I want to know what business *functions* will be present in the conference room. Beyond the demographic variables, I have found (and research supports) that functional responsibility provides some pretty good indicators of decision style, personality types, and learning preferences.[3] Accounting/finance people think differently than marketing/sales people. Human resource professionals have a different view of the world compared to information technology people. If I'm presenting to a room full of accounting/finance people, I'm going to hit the numbers hard, and the details better be right. For marketing/sales, the emphasis will be on relationships and kinesthetic activities. For human resources folks, the focus will be about the decision's impact on their people. I will talk flow charts with the information technology group, and process improvement with the production managers. For the senior operations executives, I will go to the bottom line (quickly).

For most persuasive situations that require commitment of resources and involvement

Tips from the Experts:
Put your audience first. Start by thinking about what you need to do to persuade them, not what you want to put on your first slide.

Josh Gordon
Presentations that Change Minds

across functions, you can expect a good representation of the various business functions in the room, as is the situation for the corporate benefits committee in our case study. Therefore, you have to be inclusive in your approach, designing a presentation that speaks to the needs and interests, as well as the personalities, of the different functions. That said, I still want to learn all I can about who is going to be in the room, especially the decision makers and thought leaders. If possible, I want to meet with each individually. I am interested in their individual knowledge about the topic and their disposition (pro or con) toward my idea. I want to know the issues uppermost on their mind and about any "hot buttons" they are bringing into the room. I need to understand how they like to make decisions. In some cases, for larger audiences, I might even design a research or data collection questionnaire.[4]

Kitty Locker, author of *Business and Administrative Communication*, calls this approach "you-attitude," when you put yourself in the audience's shoes, look at issues from an audience's point of view, emphasize what the audience wants to know, and respect the audience's experience and intelligence.[5]

In a persuasive situation, I cannot overemphasize the importance of conducting pre-presentation interviews with representative members of the audience. In addition to building rapport and uncovering potential objections, you can sometimes gain pre-meeting buy-in on the assumptions and numbers underlying your position, enhancing the participants' "ownership" in the success of your presentation.

Returning to our case situation, Carson discussed the issues with his boss and talked with some peers who had presented to the committee. He then decided to conduct face-to-face interviews with the functional heads in his region to get a sense of how each function viewed the idea of TRPs. Figure 1.1 provides an edited synopsis of quotes from Carson's interviews plus a clip of the *chief executive officer's* (CEO's) comments from a magazine interview.

After reading the comments, you can see the power of the information gleaned from the respondents, both positive and negative. Their thoughts will help Carson shape the answers to the remaining communication strategy analysis questions.

John Walden, Regional VP of Distribution and Transportation

- "I think this push to hire people with college degrees and trying to send our current staff back to school is a mistake. Even though we're using computers a lot more, it's still pretty basic – receive, store, pick, ship, drive a truck. Plus the college kids come with a sense of entitlement. They want too much money and are not willing to put in the time it takes to pay their dues. Extra benefits like tuition reimbursement will just raise our costs."
- "I think, instead of putting in a lot of fancy, schmancy benefits, we just need to raise the pay rates. That's what keeps people hustling—cold, hard cash."

Larry Monney, Regional VP of Marketing and Sales Operations

- "There's consolidation going on in the supermarket industry. A lot of foreign-owned companies are buying and putting together regional chains. The new owners and managers are more sophisticated and financially driven. The days of sitting on a case of Tide in the back room of a store and schmoozing about baseball with the owner are long gone. Now our selling is much more consultative–figuring out how we can adapt our systems and services to meet the needs of the customer. And the selling is more on the board room level. So, yes, we are in the process of upgrading our marketing and business development teams; we're now seeking people with at least some college background."
- "On the other hand, the retail merchandising and service portion of the business has not changed too much. It requires a lot of people skills, a strong work ethic, and plenty of common sense to work with supermarket employees at the retail level. The hours can be long too. I can't imagine retail service employees finding the time or energy to use a tuition refund program to go back to school. They are more interested in incentive plans and vacation time."

Brenda Smith-Jones, Regional VP of Purchasing and Merchandising

- "The nature of our department has really changed. We use to be just buyers, beating up the vendors for every penny we could shake out of them. Now we're using sophisticated computer forecasting models and applying activity-based costing to determine the true cost of buying, warehousing, and distributing an item. Plus, we've become responsible for preparing merchandising plans for our customers."
- "We need more people with good analytical and critical thinking skills, as well as a knack for quantitative analysis. I'm encouraging my staff to get more education both at the college level and through public seminars and workshops. A tuition reimbursement program would be a big help."

Figure 1.1. Quotes from interviews with Serv-Pro regional executives about TRP.

Abbreviations: TRP, Tuition Reimbursement Plan; VP, Vice President.

Ronald Lewis, Regional VP of Information Systems

- "We've built our shop from the ground up and do all our own programming. We have a strong internal training and mentoring program and prefer to train our own programmers and technical staff, although we do hire occasionally from the local technical school. Our vendors also supply courses and workshops for free. So, from my point of view, offering to pay tuition for college courses is really not that relevant. If we have some extra money in the budget for that type of thing, I'd rather spend it on some hardware."

Reese Engle, Regional Financial Manager

- "Good finance and accounting staff are getting harder and harder to find—too few accountants, too many employers driving up wages. Plus, the new laws and regulations, such as Sarbanes-Oxley, are killing us. I've moved some administrative personnel into line positions just to fill the gaps."
- "I think an educational assistance plan would be a big help. I'd love to send some of my long-term administrative staff who are good with numbers to our local university to get an accounting degree. I also think the plan would help us in recruiting supervisory-level personnel."

Susan Rhome, Senior VP of Human Resources

- "The operating executives will have two issues with TRP. The first is the added cost. The second is retention. They will be concerned that we'll help pay for an employee's degree and then the employee will move on to what he or she considers to be bigger and better things. Unfortunately, wholesale/retail distribution is not considered to be a very glamorous field. We don't have a lot of college educated people in this industry. The executives will also be wondering how people are going to find the time to take advantage of such a benefit. Everyone is pretty maxed out just keeping up with the day-to-day workload."
- "The key question to me: Is tuition reimbursement the best use of our limited funds? You can only spend so much on payroll and benefits. What are other companies in our industry doing in regard to tuition reimbursement? Would it make a difference in recruitment and retention? What's something like this program going to cost us and what can we expect in return? What's the payback?"

Sarah Corvis, CEO (Excerpt from an interview with *Forbes* magazine)

- "We face all the typical challenges of a fast-growing business—maintaining quality, keeping costs under control, and staffing. But we really have no choice but to grow. The specialty food industry is going through consolidation, just like our supermarket customer base. Now two companies with national scope and size are putting pricing pressure on us. So, if I had to rank the issues, I'd say getting unnecessary costs out of the system so we can live with lower margins is what keeps me up at night. But I know we have a talented management team, and we'll come up with innovative ways to stay competitive."

Figure 1.1. (Continued).

What Are the Contextual Factors?

Contextual factors have to do with what is going on in the environment that may affect how the audience receives and responds to your message. The context includes the physical setting where you are presenting, circumstances in the organization, and even external events, such as news about the economy.

Concerning the physical setting, which of the following would you prefer?

- An audience assembled immediately after lunch, squeezed into an undersized room with elbow-to-elbow seating, and an LCD projector on the conference table blowing hot air on some of the participants, or
- An audience meeting at 10:00 a.m., comfortably seated in an airy, well-appointed room with rear-projection audiovisual equipment?

Obviously, you would prefer the second option. The point is that the adverse conditions in the first scenario could impair the audience's willingness to listen to you or accept your ideas. In most cases, the elements of the physical setting will be beyond your control, but if you can know in advance about difficulties with the physical setting, you can often make some adjustments in your presentation design, such as the type of visual support you select or the nature of activities that you plan to insure audience engagement. We'll talk more about the physical setting in the chapter on preparation.

As for the organizational context, you want to be aware of circumstances that may influence the disposition of the audience. Is the company prosperous or going through hard times? Will the implementation timetable you have in mind conflict with the organization's peak business season? Is there a morale problem in the organization? Is there political infighting among the functions in the room? Where is the power in the organization?

We can see some examples of contextual factors in the Serv-Pro case. The company's margins are under pressure due to competitive price-cutting, and larger retailers are pressuring manufacturers to ship direct.

The CEO has publicly stated that "getting unnecessary costs out of the system so we can live with lower margins is what keeps me up at night." And here's Carson, proposing to implement a new program that will obligate the company to pay tuition for employee schooling!

On the other hand, the company is implementing a new strategy, making the transition from being a traditional wholesaler to a logistics firm supplying services that are more sophisticated. Attention to human capital has to be part of the equation.

Given these contextual factors, it's clear that Carson's persuasive approach has to be premised on how a TRP could actually *save* the company money by helping "get unnecessary costs out of the system" caused by excessive turnover (quoting the CEO may be a useful tactic). Carson is also going to have to demonstrate how his ideas support the company's strategic direction.

Finally, you have to think about the external environment. What is going on in the news related to the economy, interest rates, the regulatory climate, and trends such as globalization? Do any of these factors affect the company or the people that will be in the room? To answer this question, draw on your experience and common sense. Read business periodicals such as *The Wall Street Journal* and *Fortune.* Tune in to the company's website and social media. Talk to people in the know. Then think about how can you adapt what you say or how you say it to accommodate what is on people's minds.

What Information Do You Need to Include?

What information do you need to include in your presentation to accomplish your purpose? What information does your audience need to make a decision or take action? Think about the three or four key points that will form the body of your presentation.

Returning to our case study, after some thought, Carson boiled his presentation down to the following narrative:

- Explain the cost of turnover, providing some credible numbers.
- Demonstrate how TRPs can help reduce turnover.
- Show that employees view TRP as a highly desirable benefit.

- Illustrate how costs can be predicted and managed with proper program design and controls.
- Explain how a TRP program supports the new company strategy.

This exercise provides a blueprint for the research that Carson will need to conduct to fill in the supporting details. For example, Carson will find that an Internet search on the "cost of employee turnover" provides a number of formulas for calculating turnover cost in a credible way. He will need to identify similar companies who have TRPs and interview them about their experience, including impact on retention. In addition, a database search through Carson's trade association, the Society for Human Resource Management (SHRM), may uncover some empirical research on the benefits of TRPs. He can review the company's recent Employee Attitude Survey, which included a section on benefit options, to document employee interest in TRPs.

What Are the Benefits to Your Audience?

You must learn to think about what your audience wants, not just what you want. All of us listen to the same radio station: WIIFM (What's in it for me?). To get people to adopt your ideas, you have to think about your audience's answer to that question.

Therefore, it is helpful to think about the benefits to your audience if they take the action you recommend and highlight those benefits at the appropriate points in your presentation, especially in your closing.

Presenters often confuse benefits with features and advantages. Table 1.2 provides a brief "sales training" tutorial on what is called the Features-Advantages-Benefits, or FAB, model.

WIIFM
"what's in it for me?"

The tutorial uses one of Serv-Pro's services for the retailer as an example.

Given the example, what does the retailer really desire? Not piece-quantity shipments but satisfied shoppers (higher sales) and a better return on investment. Those are the benefits in the eyes of the customer. Everything else is just a means to that end.

Table 1.2. The Difference Between Features, Advantages, and Benefits

Component	Describes	Serv-Pro business example
Feature	Facts or characteristics of a product or service	We ship in unit-piece quantities instead of cases
Advantage	How a feature can be used or can help a buyer	Allows more variety on the shelf and reduces inventory on the shelf
Benefit	How a feature and advantage meet a need or desire	Increases sales by satisfying the shopper's needs for variety and improves return on capital and space

So, what are the members of the Serv-Pro Benefits Committee buying? How does a TRP meet their needs and desires? What is in it for them? Here are Carson's preliminary thoughts:

- Everyone in the room is concerned about reducing costs. Excessive turnover is a huge hidden cost. If Carson can show that TRP helps reduce turnover, he can quantify the savings net of the cost. Saving money is a benefit.
- When the company loses a valued employee, it loses his or her tacit knowledge, the experience about customers and systems that's not in the procedure manuals. This loss of knowledge affects service to the customer. Taking care of the customer is part of Serv-Pro's culture and central to the company's new service strategy. TRP will benefit the new strategy by helping retain and equip current employees and recruit new employees capable of supporting the more sophisticated approach to business.
- The opportunity to take courses with TRP assistance includes the people on the committee. Many of them may be feeling a need to

> **Tips from the Experts:**
> The fool tells me his reasons, but the wise man persuades me with my own.
> Aristotle
> *The Art of Rhetoric*

upgrade their knowledge and skills in such a highly competitive and changing environment. TRP could be a valued benefit to members of the committee.

What Are the Potential Objections?

Finally, you need to think about potential objections you will have to address or minimize. Table 1.3 shows a recap of Carson's initial thoughts on potential objections gleaned from his interviews.

Having "primed his pump" with the eight questions, Carson is now ready to begin the design of the presentation to the Serv-Pro Benefits Committee. Remember, this is an iterative process. Carson will return to the questions periodically as he conducts his research and designs his presentation. He will begin by constructing the opening.

Table 1.3. Identification of Potential Objections and Responses

Potential objections	How to address or minimize
We are proposing to add a costly program cost in a time of declining margins.	Provide a cost–payback analysis based on credible research.
Employees will leave the company after we pay for their degree.	Include a vesting policy that requires a pay-back of funds if employee leaves early.
Employees don't have time to pursue college courses, given their workload.	This time issue may be true for certain departments and job categories, but most salaried/knowledge workers have indicated a desire to take courses.

Takeaways

Conducting a Communication Strategy Analysis

- Use the eight questions to inform the strategy for your presentation and guide your supporting research:
  1. What is the problem you are trying to solve?
  2. What is the purpose or outcome you want to achieve?
  3. What is your central message?
  4. Who is your target audience, and how do they make decisions?
  5. What are the contextual factors that may influence your message?
  6. What information do you need to include to build support for your position?
  7. What are the benefits to your audience?
  8. What potential objections will you need to address or minimize?
- Effective presenters are always audience-centered, connecting in meaningful ways with the audience's goals, values, and interests. Put your audience first and use "you-attitude."
- Research, research, research. Draw from your own knowledge and experience, talk with your boss, interview audience members, search the Internet and social media, read relevant business publications, and use the library databases.

CHAPTER 2

Constructing the Presentation Opening

We eventually sold our family business to a national company, which led to a position as Senior Vice President and the Chief Learning Officer for one of the company's divisions. As a senior executive in a large corporation, I attended hundreds of conference room presentations. Come with me to one of those meetings. Pretend you are the presenter.

As I take my seat, I have a lot of things on my mind: the unfinished business in the meeting I just left, the memo I need to send to my staff this afternoon, my boss's latest e-mail asking for some data I do not have, and a concern about the traffic to the airport that afternoon. In other words, I'm already distracted. I'm also wondering about your upcoming presentation. How long are you going to take? Will your delivery be another "death by PowerPoint" experience? What are your credentials?

You have about 2 minutes to gain my attention, demonstrate you are in command of the podium and your content, and convince me that your topic is meaningful to me personally. Otherwise, I am gone. I will still be there, of course. Nevertheless, I am mentally somewhere else. Without a strong opening, you may even find others surreptitiously doing a little e-mail or texting under the table while you are talking.

The above scenario is the reality of presenting in a corporate environment. Everyone is dealing with information overload, multiple deadlines, and a myriad of distractions. Therefore, the first few minutes of your presentation are critical. You must gain the attention of your audience, clarify your purpose and the benefits, and provide an overview of your agenda—all in a manner that establishes your credibility, creates rapport, and sets a positive tone for the presentation.

In the following sections, we will examine each of the opening components in turn, focusing on developing the content—*what* we want to say. We will deal with the all-important delivery—*how* we say it—in a later chapter.

Gain Attention

To break through all the distractions, open your presentation with a "hook"—a device for dramatically capturing your audience's attention. To brainstorm possible openers that will gain the attention and interest of your audience, consider using a

- rhetorical or thought question;
- relevant anecdote or story;
- startling statistic; or a
- meaningful quotation.[1]

What you do not want to do is try to open with a joke (always risky) or apologize for being unprepared or for equipment issues; it diminishes your credibility. When presenting to decision makers, if you are not serious about the topic or not prepared, you should not be there.

Each of the four methods can set the stage for a transition into your purpose statement. Returning to our case study, here are some examples created by Carson Rodrequez for the Tuition Reimbursement Plan (TRP) presentation:

- Thought question: *Have you ever thought about what employee turnover is costing our company?*

  Transition: *I think you'll be surprised when you hear the answer.*
- Relevant anecdote or story: *This is Mary (show photo), a customer service representative who recently left our company. When Mary left, she took something of value. No, it wasn't a stapler, or something like that. It was her 5 years of experience and her intimate knowledge of our customer's needs.*

  Transition: *Lately, we've had too many Marys leave the company.*
- Startling statistic: *Here's an important number: $585,000. The number represents the cost of excessive turnover in the southern region last year.*

  Transition: *The number doesn't appear anywhere on our P&L statement, but it is a cost that's very real and a threat to our new strategy.*
- Meaningful Quotation: *Here's a quote from our CEO during a recent interview with Forbes magazine:*

"So, if I had to rank the issues, I'd say getting unnecessary costs out of the system so we can live with lower margins is what keeps me up at night. But I know we have a talented management team, and we'll come up with innovative ways to stay competitive."

Transition: *I'd like to share with you today an innovative way to take unnecessary costs and help the company stay competitive.*

Clarify Purpose and Benefits

Your attention-getting opening should tie to the central point of your presentation and set the stage for your purpose statement. You want to be explicit about why you are there today, what you hope to accomplish,

> **Tips from the Experts:**
> Gear your elevator speech toward solving your audience's problems.
> Nick Morgan
> *Give Your Speech, Change the World*

and why the audience should care. Some call this approach an "elevator speech" in the sense that it is very short and focused—just three or four sentences. Here is a vignette based on our case study to help illustrate the "elevator speech" concept:[2]

Heading to his presentation, Carson Rodrequez is getting on the first floor elevator at corporate headquarters in Chicago. The corporate offices are on the 5th floor of a multi-tenant office building. As the elevator doors begin to close, in steps a serious-looking woman that Carson recognizes as Lori Salman, the senior VP of Purchasing and a member of the Benefits Committee. Lori recognizes Carson and they exchange greetings. As the elevator heads up, she says, "I believe you are the main item on the committee agenda tomorrow." Cason answers in the affirmative. Lori responds: "I have another meeting I need to attend at the same time and have been trying to decide what to do. Why should I attend your presentation?" What Carson says in that 15-second ride to the 5th floor is his elevator speech.

So what should Carson say? Here is one version Carson developed, based on his communication strategy analysis:

> *We have a serious problem with employee turnover. The hidden cost is enormous and the on-going loss of knowledge workers endangers implementation of our new corporate strategy.*
>
> *One piece of the solution may be a new employee benefit: a Tuition Reimbursement Plan (TRP). My purpose is to present the results of our feasibility study on TRPs and to recommend a course of action.*
>
> *The bottom line is that a TRP can help your function reduce costs by improving employee retention, and it can help attract the type of employees you need to support our new strategy.*

And the elevator doors open.

In 15 seconds, Carson has gained Lori's interest. She indicates she will attend, expressing some concerns about the cost of TRP. Smiling, she says as she heads to her office, "I want to see how you can make a case for adding a new employee benefit in these tough economic times. You better be wearing body armor under that suit."

> **Tips from the Experts:**
> Make them a promise. Put their minds at rest by telling them what they will get out of listening to you.
> Nick Souter
> *Persuasive Presentations*

Carson's "elevator speech" illustrates the key elements of an opening purpose statement, given the problem–solution context. Start with a statement of the problem (turnover), then add the rhetorical purpose (report and recommend), and conclude with the benefits to the audience (reduce costs/support strategy). The purpose statement concisely sounds the theme and central message of his presentation.

Provide Agenda and Overview

Your audience is now engaged and ready to listen. The third step in your presentation opening is to provide a brief overview of your agenda that explains how you plan to approach the topic. As listeners, we all need organizers to help us follow the ideas in a presentation. The overview is also a good time to let the audience know how long your prepared remarks should take and how you would like to handle questions and discussion.

The overview provides an advanced look at the structure of your presentation. Give each topic a title and explain that you have divided the presentation body into three or four manageable topics, which you will discuss in some detail during the presentation. Here is Carson's draft of his agenda overview, including the transition sentence following his purpose/benefit statement:

> *To address this issue, I've divided the content into three manageable chunks.*
>
> *First, I will share what I've learned about our turnover problem and how turnover is impacting our organization.*
>
> *Second, I will show how a Tuition Reimbursement Plan (TRP) can help address the problem. This section will include details such as cost projections.*
>
> *Third, I will provide a summary of the benefits of a TRP and address the concerns that line managers have expressed during interviews conducted as part of the research.*
>
> *I will conclude with a specific recommendation for your consideration and a call to action.*

Wrap up the opening by setting time expectations and recommending an approach for handling questions and discussion. Conclude by seeking affirmation from the audience for your proposed approach. In the world of presentation experts, there is a variety of opinions about the best way to allocate time, control the interruptions, and manage the questions.[3] I will make a case for my preferred approach for a problem–solution presentation in a conference room environment. Ultimately, of course, the decision on how to manage questions depends on the culture of the organization and the nature of your presentation. Here's my argument:

- The benefits committee allocated Carson 1 hour on the agenda, which is typical for a topic of substance. I strongly argue that the oral presentation should be only 10 to 15 minutes, with questions and discussion following, supported by a resource document to be handed out at the conclusion of the oral portion of the presentation.
- The concept here is that your oral presentation is serving as an "executive summary." I have three reasons for the executive summary approach:
  1. Attention span. Most of us cannot maintain our concentration much longer than 10 minutes, 15 minutes maximum.
  2. The big picture. I want to make sure I am able to highlight the "big ideas" in the presentation before descending into the weeds of the details.
  3. Audience involvement. I know that audience involvement is the key to gaining a favorable decision. Meetings rarely run on time, and I can expect that I will have less than an hour. I want to spend the majority of the time in discussion, clarifying issues, and addressing concerns. Therefore, I want to keep the oral portion of the presentation short and to the point.
- The supporting document is a key element in this approach. The document could be in the form of a traditional report (with a clear index) or a "flip book," a spiral-bound collection of specially constructed PowerPoint slides that are more detailed than your presentation slides (we'll look at flip books in more detail in the chapter on visuals and media). As people ask questions, you can point them to the appropriate page in the document and manage the dialogue. I always hold the document until after the presentation (letting the audience know that it is coming). Otherwise, you lose control of the audience's attention as they dig into the details while you are trying to make your key points.

Given this approach, here is one example of how Carson could establish the protocol for the meeting:

> *To manage our discussion today, I would like to propose the following protocol for the hour allocated on the agenda:*
>
> *First, I would like to spend about 15 minutes in oral presentation to provide an executive summary.*
>
> *Then I'd like to hand out a "flip book"* [hold up] *that provides all the supporting details, join you at the table, and facilitate an in-depth discussion to address your questions and concerns.*
>
> *Of course, during the oral presentation portion, if you need understanding or clarification on a particular point, please feel free to interrupt.*
>
> *Is this approach OK with everyone?* (Wait for affirmation.)
>
> *Great! Let's begin by defining the problem.* [Transition to body of presentation.]

In addition to the benefit of allowing you a chance to maintain control over the flow of the information, taking the initiative to establish the protocol also adds to your credibility, sending the message that you are a confident professional who knows how to manage a presentation.

With a draft of the opening in place, Carson is now ready to build the body of his presentation, using the problem–solution pattern.

Takeaways

Constructing the Presentation Opening

- Construct your presentation opening with three parts: gain attention, clarify purpose and benefits, and provide an overview of the agenda. Connect each part with a clear transition statement.
- Gain attention by using one of four basic methods:
  o Rhetorical or thought question
  o Relevant anecdote or story
  o Startling statistic
  o Meaningful quotation
- Craft an "elevator speech" for your purpose/benefit statement. Explain why you are there, what you hope to accomplish, and why the audience should care. Include
  o a statement of the problem (e.g., turnover),
  o your rhetorical purpose, (e.g., report and recommend), and
  o the benefits to the audience (e.g., reduce costs).
- Provide the audience an advanced look at the topical structure of your presentation and propose a recommended protocol for your time together, for example:
  o Deliver oral presentation: 10–15 minutes.
  o Handout report or "flip book" with details, charts, and graphs.
  o Facilitate questions and discussion.

CHAPTER 3

Building the Body of the Presentation

There are three critical elements to think about as you build the body of the presentation: using the appropriate pattern of organization, selecting audience-centered content, and applying the principles of the Persuasion Triangle.

Follow a Pattern of Organization

Have you ever attended a presentation where the speaker rambled, bouncing in a seemingly random fashion from idea to idea? I bet you felt irritated and impatient, coming away with little comprehension or positive feeling about the speaker. That is why organization in the body of your presentation is so important. Unlike written documents, which have headings, topic sentences, paragraphs, lists, and indentations to signal organization and levels of detail, your audience needs explicit cues in an oral presentation to follow your ideas. These cues depend on the organization of your content and your oral transitions (often called "signposts") from topic to topic and point to point.

Experiments show that organizational structure makes a difference in the effectiveness of oral presentations.[1] Not surprisingly, when a presentation is well organized and flows coherently, listeners report greater comprehension and perceive the speaker to be more competent and trustworthy. The key is to use proven patterns of organization that relate to your purpose. Most oral presentation patterns have three parts, each containing supporting points.[2] For example, a chronological pattern is common in business presentations—past, present, and future—often phrased in the form of questions, such as "Where have we been? Where are we now? Where do we want to go?"

Given the context of our case, we have chosen to use the problem–solution pattern, which follows the flow shown in Figure 3.1.

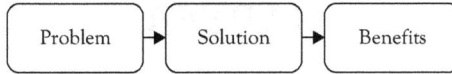

Figure 3.1. Problem–solution pattern.

Following the problem–solution pattern, you will 1) define and document the problem, 2) present your proposed solution, contrasting alternatives if appropriate, and 3) summarize the benefits, while addressing potential objections or concerns.

Develop Audience-Centered Content

Under each topic, you need to select carefully your supporting points, focusing on the information—facts, anecdotes, and documentation—most relevant to your audience and your purpose. Stick with the BIG IDEAS. Remember, the oral portion of your presentation is functioning as an executive summary.

> **Tips from the Experts:**
> Stay out of the weeds. Presenting detail after detail turns off decision makers who want the big picture. Make your subject come alive by giving examples, illustrations, and brief case studies.
>
> Robert Bly
> *Persuasive Presentations for Business*

Where we typically go wrong is to include too many details. We work so hard collecting information; we hate to leave anything out. Save most of the details for your handout. For example, the tuition reimbursement plan (TRP) issue has a tax angle. You may point out the tax treatment in your benefits section, but it would be a mistake to launch into a dissertation on the ins and outs of the tax law. Why? Because most of the decision makers do not really care about the details of the tax law. Given you have established credibility, they are interested in the application—*how* the law affects the decision. During the question-and-answer session, if you have a person in the audience who wants to know more about the tax perspective, you can point that person (and the audience) to the page in your handout that summarizes the tax regulations.

An outline, summarizing your main points, is helpful to clarify your thinking. As an example, Table 3.1 provides Carson's outline of the main

Table 3.1. Key Point Outline for Body of Presentation

What does the audience want to know?	Key point topic outline
	Problem
What's the problem?	1. Our turnover of salaried employees is significantly above the industry norm.

How does the problem impact our business?	2. The problem impacts our business two ways:
	  a. The turnover generates significant hidden costs.
	  b. The ongoing loss of knowledge workers also hinders the implementation of our new corporate strategy.

What's the root of the problem? What's causing the turnover?	3. A variety of factors affects turnover of salaried technical, professional, and managerial employees. Our exit interviews indicate three main issues:
	  a. Issues related to work–life balance and the desire for more "family-friendly" policies.
	  b. Concerns about the "leadership styles" of management.
	  c. Desires for company support in "reskilling" to meet the new demands in the marketplace.

	4. We are currently researching the first two issues and will return with recommendations in future meetings. Our purpose today is to address the reskilling issue.
	Solution
What's your solution?	1. Employee surveys and exit interviews indicate that offering a TRP as a new employee benefit is one piece of the turn-over solution.
How does a TRP work?	2. Employers reimburse employees who meet certain criteria for direct costs of coursework at accredited academic institutions.
Are other companies in our industry offering TRPs?	3. Our top three competitors offer TRPs; 85% of publicly held companies offer TRPs.
	Benefits/Objections
What are the expected benefits of a TRP?	1. Research shows that TRPs can reduce costs by improving retention. 2. A TRP can help improve the skills of current employees, improving productivity and quality of work. 3. TRPs can help attract the type of employees we need to support our new strategy as we grow. 4. The company receives favorable tax benefits for offering a TRP.

(continued)

Table 3.1. Key Point Outline for Body of Presentation (continued)

What does the audience want to know?	Key point topic outline

What are the pitfalls?	5. We've identified three main concerns about implementing a TRP:
	  a. Employees may leave the company after completing their degree.
	  b. We are adding a benefit with a potentially open-ended cost.
	  c. With current workloads, employees may not have time to attend classes.

Can we design a program to address the concerns?	6. Most TRP plans contain the following features which address the concerns:
	  a. Employee eligibility based on full-time status and length of service
	  b. Preapproval by HR and employee supervisor
	  c. Only job-related/degree-related courses from accredited institutions
	  d. Ceiling on number of courses per year or annual reimbursement dollars or both
	  e. Requirement of satisfactory course completion (A or B)
	  f. Employment agreement requiring reimbursement to company if employee leaves within a certain time period

Abbreviation: TRP, Tuition reimbursement plan.

points for the body of his TRP presentation, organized under the topical headings of the problem–solution pattern. To reinforce the importance of meeting the needs of the audience, Carson also included a column that links his content with the questions he thinks his audience would like answered. At this stage, use full sentences in the key point content outline for clarity and precision. Later in the process, you will reduce the ideas to visuals and key phrases.

Apply the Principles of the Persuasion Triangle

As you build your content to support your key points, think about ways to incorporate the elements of the Persuasion Triangle: credibility, logic, and emotional appeal. Following are some examples for each element.

Credibility

Your credibility, how the audience perceives you as the source of the message, depends on three primary factors: your relationships, your character, and your competence.[3]

Regarding relationships, we are more likely to trust people we know. That is why it is important, as noted earlier, to research your audience in advance, meet with each individual if possible, and seek areas of common interests, including personal factors such as sports or children. Perceived similarity is an important link between you and your audience. If you cannot meet with your audience in advance, arrive early for the meeting. Introduce yourself as people arrive and chat for a moment with as many as you can.

Your character is how the audience regards your sincerity, trustworthiness, and concern for their well-being and the well-being of the organization. The passion and conviction of your presentation delivery shapes some of this perception.

> **Tips from the Experts:**
> If you are unknown to your audience, the person who introduces you should lay the groundwork regarding your credentials, experience, and character.
> Jay Conger
> *The Necessary Art of Persuasion*

We will look at that delivery component in a future chapter. But your track record also shapes the perception of your character. Have you met commitments in the past? Do you "walk your talk?" Have you demonstrated dependability in a challenging situation? For example, Carson has been with the organization 12 years, came out of the line organization, moved into HR, and worked his way up the chain to Regional VP. He has led two high-profile project teams successfully and was recently a lead negotiator in contract negotiations with the company's truck drivers. He has a reputation as a tough but principled negotiator.

Your competence is how the audience perceives your expertise and knowledge of the subject. Your presentation opening lays the groundwork for your credibility by demonstrating that you are a confident professional in command of the presentation process. Now you must convince the audience that you have done your homework by providing evidence, with specific examples, to support your points and citing trustworthy sources, including empirical research when available. That leads us to the logic component.

Logic

Decision makers want numbers, especially if you are proposing a course of action that will cost money. So stay with me in this section, even if you're not a "numbers person." The following approach is what it takes if you are going to sell your argument to management.

For the TRP argument, the logic flow will include the following assertions:

1. Voluntary turnover of salaried employees at Serv-Pro is significantly above the norm.
2. The excess turnover generates a significant cost.
3. Research shows that TRPs can improve retention.
4. The amount saved in turnover costs by improving retention will be greater than the expected tuition reimbursement expenditures.

Carson will not only have to present facts, data, and financial analysis to support his argument, but will also have to interpret and draw conclusions from the evidence. For example, to say, "Turnover of salaried employees is significantly above the norm" is not enough. His audience will want to know how much above the norm, the basis for the norm, and the source of your evidence. Table 3.2 offers an example of data collected during Carson's research that provides answers to what the audience will want to know.

A conclusion Carson can draw from the data (besides that the negative trend is increasing) is that, with 325 salaried employees and given the 8 percentage points difference between Serv-Pro's turnover and the

Table 3.2. Comparative Voluntary Turnover Rate for Salaried Employees (Southern Region)

Calendar year	Employee turnover (%)	
	Serv-Pro salaried	NAWD Average*
2012	20%	12%
2011	17%	13%
2010	16%	11%

* *Source*: National Association of Wholesale Distributors Annual HR Survey

industry norm in 2012, the company lost 26 more employees than it should have (325 × 8%). This calculation provides the input for the next step in the argument. Note that, from a credibility perspective, Carson is addressing only the number of lost employees above the industry norm.

In the same manner, Carson has to quantify the cost of turnover to the organization. Fortunately, a Google search reveals numerous studies and reports on the cost of turnover.[4] The costs include elements related to separation, recruitment, hiring, training, lost productivity, and increased errors. Table 3.3 provides some examples of costs related to replacing an employee.

The Society for Human Resource Management estimates that the total turnover cost for knowledge workers and managers can range from 90% to 200% of the annual salary.[5] So, what is the salaried turnover above the norm costing Serv-Pro? Table 3.4 shows the calculations, using a conservative estimate of 50% of the annual salary. Note that Carson selected a conservative approach to build credibility.

Table 3.3. Example Costs Related to Employee Turnover

Separation Costs • HR staff time (exit interview, paperwork administration) • Accrued paid time off (vacation, sick pay) **Replacement Costs** • Management time spent recruiting, screening, and hiring • Clerical and computer costs for processing records and forms **Learning Costs** • Management time spent on orientation, training, and extra supervision • Low productivity during learning period **Other Costs During Transition** • Communication problems, errors, and mistakes • Lost business, customer dissatisfaction

Table 3.4. Estimated Annual Cost of Excess Turnover for Serv-Pro

Number of employees lost beyond industry norm	26
× 50% of average salary of $45,000	$22,500
Estimated annual cost of turnover	$585,000

The next step is to make the case that TRPs can improve retention. Again, Carson is fortunate that there are a number of empirical studies to support his argument. Table 3.5 presents summary statements from three studies that support the retention hypothesis.

Table 3.5. Excerpts from Empirical Studies on the Effect of TRP on Turnover

"Results suggest that tuition assistance plans are associated with lower rates of turnover even independent of wage effects . . . . employees stay longer to use the tuition assistance."[6]
"Employees who earned degrees through the company were 39% less likely to quit than employees who did not participate in tuition reimbursement."[7]
"Participation in tuition reimbursement substantially reduces the probability of separating from the employer within five years by nearly 50 percentage points."[8]

Abbreviation: TRP, Tuition reimbursement plan.

All of the quotes in Table 3.5 come from very credible sources, including *The Journal of Econometrics*, the *Academy of Management Journal*, and the National Bureau of Economic Research, respectively.

The final step in the logic is to project the expected annual cost of the TRP and relate that cost to the cost of turnover. Here are the facts according to Carson's research:

- According to *The Wall Street Journal*, the average employee participation in a TRP is about 10%.[9] Given the 325 employee base of Serv-Pro's Southern Region, Carson can project that about 33 employees per year will be participating.
- According to the College Board's annual report, *Trends in College Pricing*, the average in-state public college cost per 3-hour credit course is approximately $1,000, which includes tuition, fees, and books.[10] Assuming that the Serv-Pro plan limits to four the number of courses the company will pay for per year, the projected annual cost per participating employee would be about $4,000 or $132,000 per year for 33 employees.
- Given the estimated $22,500 cost to replace a salaried employee, if the program reduces the 26 employees lost above the norm by 6 employees (23%), the benefit would have a

Table 3.6. Potential Effect on Costs from a Tuition Reimbursement Plan (TRP)

	Current cost of turnover	**Reduced turnover 23%**	**Reduced turnover 40%**
Cost per employee	$ 22,500	$ 22,500	$ 22,500
Number of employees lost	26	20	16
Projected cost	585,000	450,000	360,000
Reduction in cost		135,000	225,000
Project cost of TRP		132,000	132,000
Net TRP benefit		$ 3,000	$ 93,000

slight positive net effect on cost. In other words, saving six employees will pay for the cost of the TRP. If Serv-Pro could reduce the turnover by 40% (10 employees), in line with expectations based on research, the net savings would be $93,000. Table 3.6 provides a summary of the calculations.

In the chapter on visual support, we will discuss ways to present all this data in a digestible form, with details provided in the meeting handout. At this point, Carson is simply collecting and organizing his data.

Emotional Appeal

People don't make decisions—even business decisions—on logic alone. We use our head (adding up the facts), but we also use our gut (assessing credibility) and our heart (satisfying our emotional needs). Emotional appeals—what Aristotle referred to as pathos—are intended to stir listeners' emotions, creating feelings like sadness, pride, or even fear. Emotional appeal means making the listener *want* to take action to address the emotion. So how can Carson incorporate emotional appeal in his TRP presentation?

In addition to the hidden cost, the excessive turnover at Serv-Pro is also creating another problem—hindering implementation of the new corporate strategy. The company is making the transition from being a traditional wholesaler to a more sophisticated supply chain/logistics firm.

The goal is to provide for the customers a variety of customized distribution services, technology support, and retail-level category management and merchandising services. The strategy requires upgrading the skills of current employees, as well as attracting new employees with experience in the new services being offered. Documenting this problem provides opportunity to incorporate emotional appeal into the presentation.

A growing body of research in the area of human capital links high turnover rates to shortfalls in organizational performance.[11] It makes sense when you think about it. The knowledge in an organization is in two forms: *explicit* and *tacit*. Explicit knowledge is the type that can be documented in procedure manuals. Tacit knowledge is what is in people's heads, built from experience that allows them to perform at a high level. Often, they cannot really explain how they know when and how to do certain things. When they leave the organization, their tacit knowledge leaves with them.

Closely related to tacit knowledge is the concept of *social capital*, the relationships employees have built both within and outside the firm. Outside the firm, these relationships include intimate knowledge of the needs and preferences of external stakeholders such as customers, vendors, and government agencies. Again, when an employee leaves, some of the social capital, often developed over years, goes with them.

Carson can best illustrate the importance of this problem by explaining the tacit knowledge/social capital concepts and providing an anecdote or story gleaned from his exit interviews to illustrate the impact. For example, there is Mary, a customer service representative, who left after five years with the company. Mary had excellent relationships with her assigned customers and deep knowledge of their needs. She could often anticipate problems and had a knack for calming an upset customer. Mary left because she had a strong desire to finish her college degree to advance her career but could not afford the tuition. She joined another company that offered a TRP and a path for advancement. Since Mary's departure, competitors have been able to gain a portion of business from two of her accounts. You can see how this story touches the emotions, both from sorrow over the loss of Mary and the angst caused by loss of business.

Another opportunity for emotional appeal lies in the psychological principle called *social proof*.[12] The principle of social proof states that people often decide what to believe or what action to take in a situation by looking at what other people are doing. People follow the lead of similar others. A lot of similar people following a course of action signals that it must be the right thing to do. Carson should include in his presentation that 85% of publically held firms offer a TRP.[13] By talking with his HR contacts in competitor firms, Carson also found that ServPro's top three competitors in the specialty foods distribution arena offer TRPs. The two facts together should serve as powerful and persuasive social proof.

Another psychological principle is *authority*.[14] People defer to experts who provide shortcuts to decisions requiring specialized information. We have already seen this principle applied through the use of credible resources such as the *Journal of Econometrics* and *Academy of Management Journal* to document empirical research on the effect of TRPs on reducing turnover. The same empirical studies also reinforce the assertion that TRPs help support the recruitment process. Table 3.7 provides two example quotes from the literature.

One of the recognized authorities on influence and the psychological principles of persuasion is Robert Ciadini, author of *Influence: Science and Practice*. In his book and in several *Harvard Business Review* articles, Ciadini lays out principles of persuasion that relate to emotional appeal and the presentation context. Table 3.8 provides a brief synopsis of his six principles of persuasion.[17]

I recommend that you read Ciadini's work to learn more about the nuances of emotional appeal. Effective and ethical use of emotional appeal can be a powerful motivator that moves your audience to take action.

With a draft of the presentation body in place, Carson is now ready to put together a strong conclusion. The next chapter will show how to close with power.

Table 3.7. Excerpts from Empirical Studies on the Effect of TRP on Recruitment

"Workers who have higher ability and motivation self-select into firms with tuition assistance plans."[15]
"Offering tuition reimbursement affects the type of worker attracted to the firm."[16]

Abbreviation: TRP, Tuition reimbursement plan.

Table 3.8. Ciadini's Six Principles of Persuasion

Principle	Description	Presentation application
Liking	If people like you—because they sense you like them or because of things you have in common—they're more likely to say yes to your requests.	Interview audience members in advance or chat with them before the presentation. Seek to discover common interests. Make sincere positive remarks about them or the organization.
Reciprocity	People tend to return favors. If you help people, they'll help you. If you behave co-operatively, they'll respond in kind.	After an interview, follow-up with a thank-you note and additional information of interest, such as a relevant article from a trade publication.
Social proof	We determine what is best by finding out what other people similar to us think is best.	Identify other companies or esteemed individuals who are already doing what you propose.
Consistency	People want to be consistent. If they make a public, voluntary commitment, they tend to follow through.	Suggest a trial period or a pilot project. If accepted, you've convinced the audience to agree in principle.
Authority	People defer to experts and those in positions of authority	Cite research from credible sources or provide quotes from recognized authorities to support your argument.
Scarcity	People value things more if they perceive them to be scarce or exclusive.	Emphasize the size of the loss if your recommendation is not followed. Limit the window of action and provide a reason for acting quickly.

Takeaways

Building the Body of the Presentation

- Use the problem–solution pattern to organize your presentation body.
  - Problem: Define and document the problem.
  - Solution: Present your proposed solution (contrast alternatives if appropriate).
  - Benefits: Summarize the benefits while addressing potential objections or concerns.
- Develop audience-centered content.
  - Answer the questions on the minds of your audience.
  - Speak to their needs and problems. What keeps them up at night?
  - Stick with the BIG IDEAS; avoid information overload.
  - Use facts, stories, testimonies, and documentation that are relevant to your audience and purpose.
- Integrate the principles of the Persuasion Triangle throughout your presentation.
  - Establish credibility through relationships, by your character, and competence; demonstrate your expertise, knowledge, and use of trustworthy sources.
  - Use logic and clear presentation/interpretation of facts, data, and financial analysis to support your argument. If you're proposing to spend money, you must demonstrate a payback.
  - Incorporate emotional appeal though stories and psychological principles like social proof and authority.

CHAPTER 4

Closing with Power

After 32 years in the corporate world, I retired to academia to teach, research, and consult. As in business, persuasive presentations are a part of work life on a university campus. I recently attended a presentation aimed at convincing our faculty to commit time and resources to starting an MBA partnership with a university in China. After presenting his case, the speaker concluded abruptly, taking us by surprise. Even in casual conversation, you expect some signal that the talk is ending. Such a sudden ending left the audience puzzled and unfulfilled.

Remember that the impressions from your closing words will probably linger in your audience's minds. You want to leave a strong final impression. Therefore, you need to design your conclusion with as much care as the introduction. Your transition from the body of the presentation should provide an audible signal that you are moving to a conclusion (e.g., "In conclusion," or "I'd like to conclude by . . . ."). You can also let your audience know the end is in sight by your manner of delivery, such as moving away from the podium and toward the audience or by changing the tone, pacing, and intonation of your voice. With your audible signal and change in delivery, attention from your audience will immediately increase.

Like the introduction, the closing includes three steps: summarizing the big ideas, calling the audience to action, and ending on a memorable note. Make the closing concise and to the point, not more than two or three minutes long. It's time to "close the deal" and "ask for the order."

Summarize the Big Ideas

Begin the conclusion by explicitly restating the central idea and main points of your presentation, with emphasis on the benefits of your solution. Using our tuition reimbursement plan (TRP) example, Carson's summary will incorporate the elements of his elevator speech and might sound something like this:

In summary, we have a serious problem with employee turnover. The hidden cost is enormous and the ongoing loss of knowledgeable workers endangers implementation of our new corporate strategy.

One piece of the solution is a Tuition Reimbursement Plan (TRP). I've demonstrated that a TRP can help reduce turnover and the cost of the entire TRP can be more than offset through the savings from reduced turnover. Saving just six employees per year will pay for the cost of the TRP.

In addition, a TRP not only helps upgrade the skills of our current employees but also helps attract and retain the type of employees we need to support our new strategy. Remember, workers who have higher ability and motivation self-select into firms with tuition assistance plans. We are competing for those employees against companies who already offer TRPs.

Finally, I'm confident we can design a program that addresses the typical concerns and issues about TRPs, such as controlling the upside cost and retention after completion of a degree or certificate.

Call the Audience to Action

Persuasion has a selling context. You're trying to convince an audience to buy your ideas. Sales professionals are taught to explicitly "ask for the order" as part of closing the deal. We're at that point in the persuasive business presentation.

After summarizing the big ideas of the presentation, ask for the action you want in a direct manner. Be specific. Make the action a realistic next step and suggest a timeline, giving a reason to act promptly.

Continuing our TRP example, here is Carson's version of a call to action:

So today, I am asking for your permission and support to conduct a 2-year pilot of a Tuition Reimbursement Plan in the Southern region to evaluate the benefits, costs, and pitfalls of a TRP.

To get started, the project would involve the following action steps with the indicated timeline:

1. *Form a TRP policy project team representative of the business functions (by January 31).*
2. *Draft a TRP policy and procedures document tailored to Serv-Pro's needs (by March 15).*
3. *Submit the TRP document to the Benefits Committee for approval (for April meeting).*
4. *Communicate to Southern Region employees the availability of the TRP (during the month of May).*

May is a good target date for implementation because that allows employees to plan for registration for the fall semester. Classes normally begin in mid-August for most schools. To make this timeline, I hope to have your approval today after the conclusion of our discussion.

You may feel that asking for a decision from your audience in such a direct manner is too aggressive. But remember your purpose. A persuasive presentation has a clear goal. It makes no sense to leave your audience without clearly asking for what you want. The key is to ask respectfully but with confidence.

As Carson's example illustrates, make it easier for the decision makers to say "yes" by being very specific and asking for a realistic next step. In Carson's case, the request is for a "pilot program" in a single region. He clearly outlined the action steps required. Proposing a pilot reduces the risk for the company and sets up what is essentially a research project to provide company-specific data on the costs and benefits of a TRP. If nothing else, the curiosity factor—the desire to see if Carson's data checks out—will help motivate the audience to agree. Notice also that the timeline includes an opportunity for the committee to meet with Carson to review the actual TRP policy prior to going public with the program, another safety valve for the decision makers.

The timeline also gives Carson a reason for asking the committee to act promptly on his request, that is, to synchronize with the next college registration cycle. The longer the committee delays the decision, the more likely other competing needs will distract, making it less likely that they will take action on Carson's proposal. After the discussion, in the event that the committee decides to defer the decision, Carson should press for a decision target date. Locker and Kaczmarek, in their book *Business Communication*, suggest three ways to remind the audience why you need a quick response:[1]

1. Show that the time limit is real. In Carson's case, this requirement means emphasizing the college registration cycle.
2. Show that acting now will save time or money. For Serv-Pro, reducing turnover, as demonstrated by Carson's data, saves money.
3. Show the cost of delaying action. Delay will not only mean more unnecessary costs due to turnover, but it also affects the company's ability to execute its new strategy.

Close with Power

Finally, close your presentation with grace and power, ending on a strong, memorable note. Be creative in devising a conclusion that hits the hearts and minds of your audience. I usually select from three basic options: ending with a relevant quotation, linking back to the introduction, or telling a "vision" story.

Close with a Quotation

The closing quotation is a relatively easy technique. The quote should meet four criteria: 1) relevant to the presentation, 2) short, 3) memorable, and 4) from a recognized, credible source. For example, Carson might use one of my favorite quotes from Jack Welch, the former CEO of General Electric: "The team with the best players wins."[2] With this quote on the screen, Carson could say:

> *In conclusion, I'd like to close with this quote from Jack Welch: "The team with the best players wins." That's really the bottom line. For Serv-Pro to execute its new strategy and win in the marketplace, we need the best players. A TRP will help us attract and retain those players.*

Link Back to Your Opening

A second approach, which gives your presentation psychological unity, is to conclude by linking back to the introduction. For example, if Carson used a startling statistic in the opening, such as last year's hidden cost of turnover in the Southern Region ($585,000), he could put that number back on the screen and say something like this:

> *In closing, here's the number I opened the presentation with: $585,000. As I've demonstrated, this is a hidden loss from employee turnover in the Southern Region that's very real. Without action, the loss is only going to get larger. Let's test the TRP approach to see how much we can reduce this loss and help the company stay competitive.*

This example uses a persuasive principle called "loss aversion"—the idea that people are more motivated to avoid losses than to acquire gains.[3] Framing a choice as leading to a loss versus a gain creates a sense of stress. For example, a study, reported in *The Wall Street Journal*, presented a group of executives with a proposal for an information technology project.[4] Twice as many in the group approved the proposal when the company was predicted to lose $500,000 if the proposal was not accepted, compared to a scenario that predicted the project would lead to a profit of $500,000. Think about the message you are sending. Could you make a stronger closing by describing the potential losses as opposed to just talking about the benefits?

Use a "Vision Story"

A third approach is to close with what consultant Claudyne Wilder calls a "vision" story.[5] You tell a vision about what will happen in the future if your recommendation is approved. Your goal is to get the audience excited by the vision you create. Here is one approach Carson might use (with a photo of highly motivated and excited employees on the screen and a title "Mary and Mark and Many More"):

> *In closing, just imagine the motivational impact on our employees when they can begin to fulfill their educational dreams with the help of a tuition reimbursement plan. We've lost Mary. There's nothing we*

can do to bring her back. But there are a lot more talented Marys and Marks in our company who will benefit and more who will join our company in the future.

And think of the impact on our company—sending employees back to school will improve employee retention, help recruit higher level skills, and help our company adapt to an increasingly competitive marketplace. Given this scenario, I'm even more excited for our future!

Note also the tie-in with the Mary story used in the body of the presentation.

Of course, these three approaches are not mutually exclusive. You can often combine two or more into your closing. For example, you could open with a dramatic quotation and bring the same quotation up in the closing, building on your opening comments, perhaps even linking the quotation to a short vision story. The point is to be thoughtful and creative in how you close your presentation.

Having finished your closing, you would then distribute your handout and transition into the question and discussion portion of your presentation. Before we discuss how to manage the Q&A process, we will first work through the next section of the book devoted to delivery—how to create effective visual support, prepare for delivery, and conduct the physical delivery itself. We'll begin with Chapter 5, how to support and reinforce your content with appropriate visuals and handouts.

Takeaways

Closing with Power

- Construct your presentation closing with three parts: summarize the big ideas, call the audience to action, and end on a memorable note. Connect each part with a clear transition statement.
- Provide an audible signal (e.g., "in conclusion") and a change in delivery style to signal that you're beginning the close. Attention from your audience will immediately increase.
- Begin the conclusion by explicitly restating the central idea and main points of your presentation, with emphasis on the benefits of your solution or the losses or both that could be incurred if no action is taken.
- Ask for the action you want in a direct manner:
  - Be specific
  - Make the action a realistic next step
  - Suggest a timeline
  - Give a reason to act promptly
- Close with power, ending on a memorable note. Use one or a combination of three basic closing techniques:
  - Relevant quotation
  - Link back to the opening
  - Vision story

PART II

Delivering a Problem–Solution Presentation

CHAPTER 5

Creating Visual Support

You have been there. You are in a conference room. A project team is reporting. They have PowerPoint slides, lots of slides with lots of words on each slide. The slides are like giant note cards, and each speaker cannot resist turning his body toward the screen, reading the words, and talking to the slides. There are charts and graphs, too—loaded with colored lines and bars with tiny legends that you have to turn your head sideways to interpret. While you are trying to figure out which region is the orange line (the one with the steepest decline), you are not listening to the speaker. Your attention begins to wander, and you are feeling slightly annoyed. Afterwards, you hear the jokes from members of the audience, phrases such as "Death by PowerPoint" and "Power Pointless."

From our own experience, we know that business people have little patience for slide after slide of boring bullet points and lots of "chart junk." We also know that decision makers, in particular, prefer clean, simple slides that quickly enhance their understanding of the important points. They are interested in you, your story, and your interpretation of the big ideas, not deciphering obtuse visuals and sitting through technical circuses.

Yet, we continue to see slide presentations that distract and handouts that confuse. Why? One answer is because the software lets us. Most people do not have ready access to graphic design experts. They are on deadline and do the best they can, without being aware of some basic design principles and techniques that would save them time and enhance their presentations. In addition, we load our slides with words because we are afraid we will forget something and look foolish. Then we talk to our slides because we made them, we are comfortable with them, and they do not judge us. It feels safer to talk to the slides than to the people.[1]

Therefore, this chapter explores a few powerful principles that will help you support and reinforce your content with appropriate visuals and handouts and make it easier to talk to your audience rather than your slides. First, I will review some interesting research on how humans

> **Tips from the Experts:**
> The single most important thing you can do to dramatically improve your presentations is to have a story to tell before you work on your PowerPoint file.
>
> Cliff Atkinson
> *Beyond Bullet Points*

process and comprehend multimedia messages. Knowledge of this research will change the way you think about and design the visuals for your presentations. Second, I will share five simple principles for creating effective visuals and provide some examples. I will conclude this chapter by addressing the handout component, a key element in the question and discussion session that follows your presentation. In addition to the "takeaway" summary at the end of the chapter, I have also included an annotated list of "how to" resources on visual support for those who are interested in some technical help.

Our discussion will focus on principles and be independent of the presentation software. In addition to PowerPoint (Microsoft) and Keynote (Apple), there are a number of new presentation tools in the market, including the "zoomables," such as Prezi, which is growing in popularity. Any of the programs can create stunning presentations, and all have strengths and weaknesses. But it's not the tool, it's how you use the tool to support your message that's important. If the audience is amazed at your use of nifty software, you are focusing on the wrong thing.

How People Process Words and Visuals

In his book, *Multimedia Learning*, Richard Mayer pulls together the research on how human brains process verbal and visual media.[2] His cognitive theory of multimedia learning provides important insights into the design of visual support for our presentations. Although Mayer's theory can be somewhat complex, the following paragraphs summarize the elements most relevant to our business presentation context.[3]

Humans have two separate information channels in the brain for auditory and visual processing.[4] Presentations target these processing systems through two of our senses, the eyes and the ears. The ears serve as the delivery path for the presenter's oral narrative, processing in the *auditory/verbal channel* in the brain. The eyes serve as the delivery path image on the screen processes in a separate area of the brain, called the *visual/pictorial channel*. According to Mayer, "In the process of building the connections between words and picture, learners are able to create a deeper understanding than from words or pictures alone."[5]

The problem occurs when we put words on the screen in the form of sentences or long bullet points. The processing of the text goes through the eyes into the visual/pictorial channel of the brain. Then the words transfer to the auditory/verbal center of the brain for translation. Do you see the problem? Each channel has a limited capacity for processing. While you are talking, sending messages through my ears to my brain's verbal channel, I am also simultaneously trying to read and translate the text on the screen, working extra hard moving the text through the visual channel to the verbal channel center. The result is verbal and cognitive overload! *I cannot read what is on the screen and listen to you at the same time.* Thinking about this phenomenon is sobering. By putting a lot of text on the screen, we are actually making it harder for the audience to follow and understand our presentation.

So what are the implications of Mayer's research for presenters? The answer is that we need to design the visual support for our presentations in the light of how the human mind works. Use pictures to reinforce your verbal points and minimize or eliminate words on the screen. If you want to include a word or two with the picture, make it short and descriptive, reinforcing the slide's message (Figure 5.1). Give the audience a moment

Figure 5.1. Use images to convey your message and minimize the words.

to process the slide, then elaborate on your point. If you must use bullet points, keep them short and progressively disclose each one using the PowerPoint animation function. Otherwise, people are reading ahead, processing all the words on the screen and not listening to you.

One of my top MBA students provided a good example application of Mayer's research. She developed a persuasive presentation aimed at senior adults. The purpose was to persuade seniors to incorporate at least 30 minutes of brisk walking into their daily activity. After making the case for walking as a beneficial exercise, she provided some examples of how the seniors could incorporate more walking into their week. She could have supported her presentation with a bullet point slide, containing, for example, three points:

- Park your car further from the entrance to the grocery store
- Take the stairs instead of the elevator
- Put your car in the garage; then walk back to the mail box

Instead, she used three photos, each a separate slide, showing a car parked a distance from the store entrance, stairs adjacent to an elevator, and a mailbox at the end of a driveway. In other words, she "spoke" the bullet points, elaborating as appropriate, and she reinforced her words with the images on the screen. She closed with another full-screen photograph, showing an elderly gentleman holding his granddaughter's hand as they walked down a country path. She told a story of how her grandfather had taken her along for his daily "constitution" walk when she was a little girl and the memories that made. The message was clear and meaningful, touching the hearts of her target audience.

We can apply the same principles to our Serv-Pro presentation. For example, one of Carson's possible "hooks" for his presentation opening was to raise the issue of the cost of employee turnover by posing a thought question. The supporting image could be an employee leaving through a revolving door, with the word "Cost of Turnover?" on the screen (Figure 5.2). After posting the slide, Carson might say:

Have you ever thought about what the revolving door of employee turnover is costing our company? (Pause.)

Figure 5.2. Use images to reinforce the message.

I think you will be surprised when you hear the answer.

My purpose today is . . . .

The same approach applies to data slides, including tables and charts. We have a tendency to overload the slide with information. A common issue, for example, is to put a bar chart on the screen showing multiple columns, in multiple colors, over multiple periods with a little legend on the side that keys the various colors. Again, I cannot decipher the slide and listen to you at the same time. The handout is the place for this level of detail. Any table or chart designed for the oral presentation needs to be big and simple—intended to reinforce a specific point.

> **Tips from the Experts:**
> Data slides are not really about the data. They are about the meaning of the data.
>
> Nancy Duarte
> *Slide:ology*

With a transition sentence, introduce and project the slide on the screen, then pause. Your audience should be able to look at the slide and, within two or three seconds, comprehend the message in the data. Then they can turn their attention back to you for interpretation, explanation, and analysis.

Figure 5.3 provides an example chart designed to support Carson's point that turnover of salaried employees at Serv-Pro is significantly above the norm and trending the wrong way.

Serv-Pro's Turnover Gap
Salaried Employees (%)

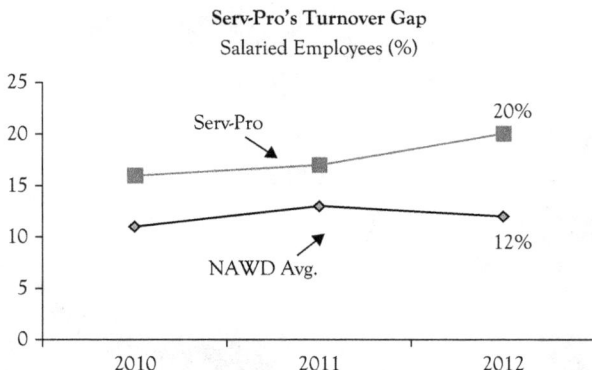

Figure 5.3. Keep charts big and simple.

Abbreviation: NAWD, National Association of Wholesale Distributors.

Remember, the presentation is about your ideas and the needs of the audience, not your slides. The visuals should help support and reinforce your key points. That is all they are meant to do.

The Five C's of Visual Support

To help keep your visuals big, bold, simple, and easy for your audience to comprehend, follow the "Five C's"—my basic principles for visual support.

1. *Concentration*: Each visual should represent one idea and support a specific point you want to make.

   For example, I recently attended a presentation where the presenter was reporting on survey responses about a change in tipping policy for a restaurant chain. It was an opinion survey of three different groups—employees, customers, and managers. For the key question in the survey (an agree/disagree, not sure response), the presenter put up a slide showing three sets of bar charts representing the number of responses for each group for each option. It was too much information to digest at a glance. While she talked about the employee response, I found myself looking at the customer data bars, which had a very high number of disagrees, and thinking about the implications. I stopped listening to the presenter.

Following the concentration principle, the better approach would be a separate slide for each reporting group, allowing the presenter to interpret the data and draw conclusions for the audience before discussing the results of the next group. At the end of the series, the presenter could then provide a summary conclusion about the overall survey data. In addition, a pie chart with percentages would be a better chart type, making it easier to interpret visually (Figure 5.4).

Customers Oppose 18% Service Charge

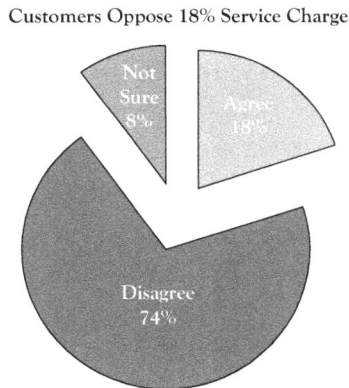

Figure 5.4. Focus on one point and reduce the chart to essentials.

In Figure 5.4, note that the chart has been stripped to its essentials. The title communicates the message of the slide. I removed the legend and incorporated the text into the pie slices. The pie colors are logical for the data and subliminally support the message. The disagree pie is red (stop), agree is green (go), and the "not sure" pie is gray, for neutral. Avoid three-dimensional (3D) effects, which create distortions in scale. Again, the audience should be able to quickly grasp the message of the chart and then turn their attention back to the speaker for interpretation and development of the message. The slide *concentrates* on one idea and supports a specific point.

2. *Clarity*: Each visual should be perfectly clear from the back of the room; no "mice type."

You have heard people say, as they put a slide on the screen: "I know you probably can't see this." If that is the case, do not do it!

Save it for the handout. As part of being big and simple (and clear from a distance), you need to bump up your font size on any text or numbers in your slides. Here is my recommended scheme for minimum font sizes:

o 36 points for topic headers
o 32 points for bullets
o 28 points for sub-bullets

If you must use bullet points, this scheme will limit the amount of text you can put on the screen and, in the case of data tables, will force you to be very selective with any numbers you present—no more Excel spreadsheets copied into slides!

As part of clarity, keep your color scheme simple and business-like. Avoid decoration in the background of the template or in the corners (do you really need your company logo on every slide?). Given the power of today's data projectors and the preference for a lighted room, use a white background with black or dark navy letters. The white background also provides maximum flexibility for blending in photos and making color selections for charts.

> **Tips from the Experts:**
> It's O.K. to have clear space—clutter is a failure of design.
>
> Nancy Duarte
> *Slide:ology*

Finally, don't be afraid of a little "white space." You do not have to fill every inch of a slide. Give the audience some visual "breathing room."

3. *Consistency:* Each visual should be consistent in style and tone and support the overall theme and message of the presentation.

Maintain a professional look by being consistent with your type font and use of upper and lower case. For slides, use a single, legible sans-serif font, such as Arial or Verdana, along with variations in its style such as bold and italic. Titles should be title case (first letter of each major word capitalized), and bullets should be short (less than seven words), left justified, and in sentence case for readability.

Maintain consistency in image style also. We all have access to huge banks of clip art and photos, but mixing clip art cartoons of various designs and photographs of different styles and tones is a mistake. Such lack of consistency suggests the presentation has been "thrown together" in haste and undermines the professional image you want to promote.

Concerning clip art, resources, such as Microsoft Office's library of clip art, often provide a style number for a clip art "family." Once you find an image you like, you can click on the details to find the style number to use in the search box or click on a search option for "similar images." This procedure provides you a selection of topical clip art drawn by the same artist in the same style.

In the same manner, consider using a professional source, such as istockphoto.com or shutterstock.com, for photographs. When you find a photo that helps support and reinforce your specific point for a slide or the theme of your presentation, you can search for additional images from the same photographer that are congruent in setting and tone. Although the images from professional sources can be somewhat pricey compared to what is "free" in sources such as Google Images, the quality and the consistency, which contribute to the professionalism of your presentation, will be worth it.

4. *Correctness*: Double-check your visuals for correctness and accuracy.

Nothing destroys credibility more than having a six-foot image on the screen with spelling errors, grammatical miscues, typos, or math mistakes.

For example, I often see bullet point lists with faulty parallel structure, which means the bullets are not consistent with each other in tense and part of speech. Most people in your audience are not expert grammarians, but when they read a bulleted list with faulty parallel structure, they will sense that something is not quite right. Compare the two lists below. Read each bullet aloud. Which is easier to read and has more impact?

Three solutions:	Three solutions:
• Customer reps need training	• Train customer reps
• System to track customer complaints	• Track customer complaints
• Performance rewards developed	• Reward good performance

The list on the right maintains parallel structure, with each bullet beginning with a strong, active verb. The list has fewer words and reads with power and punch. Although attention to this level of detail may appear a little picky, be assured there will be at least one person in your audience who cares about issues such as grammar and spelling. To that person, the little details add up and contribute to your professional persona and credibility. In other words, the person may be thinking, "How can I trust your ideas if you do not pay attention to details like grammar and proofing your work?"

The lesson here is clear. Ask multiple associates to proof your slides.

We all have difficulty proofing our own work; we are too close to it, seeing what we meant instead of what is there.

5. *Control*: Use a variety of visual techniques to control the delivery of information and focus the attention of your audience.

The animation function in PowerPoint and other presentation software is a powerful tool. Use animation to progressively disclose bullet points when you have commentary to add to each point, preventing the audience from reading ahead.

Use animation also to build a diagram or chart, section by section, as you explain the elements. By sequencing information and bringing the audience along at a comfortable pace, you enhance understanding as you tell your story.

For example, Figure 5.5 reproduces Figure 5.3, the "Turnover Gap" slide, but with some additional information that could be added with animation. Although the initial chart itself was simple enough, after Carson explains the chart and tells the story of the data, he can reinforce the big point with animation. He can display the percentage point difference and translate the difference into the number of employees lost above the norm—the number the company should not have lost. This information sets the stage for the financial argument that follows regarding the cost of turnover.

As a word of caution, when using animation: keep it simple—dissolve, fade, or wipe will do. All the other spectacular motions such as crawls, wedges, and wheels are for amateurs who do not know

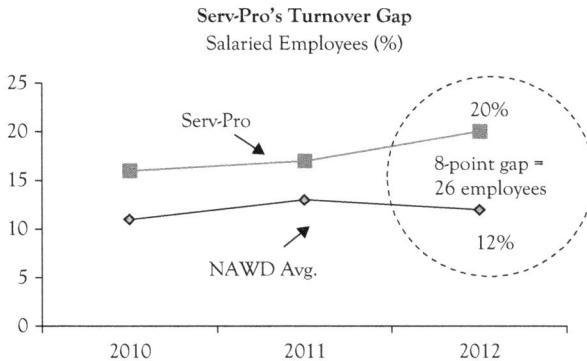

Serv-Pro's Turnover Gap
Salaried Employees (%)

Figure 5.5. Make your point with animation.

Abbreviation: NAWD, National Association of Wholesale Distributors.

any better. Use animation only to direct attention and help audience understanding; call attention to your message, not the tool.

In addition, be open and willing to experiment with other methods of controlling audience attention. For example, passing out a physical object for the audience to examine ("show and tell") can help emphasize a particular point. Sometimes, even a single-sheet handout, perhaps a drawing or illustration that works better in print than in projection, can be a way to vary the pace of the presentation and support a key idea. Remember, also, the power of a flip chart or whiteboard, which allows you to develop an idea with the audience interactively.

When you switch to other media, you need to make the screen go dark to refocus the audience's attention. For example, in PowerPoint slideshow mode, you can use the "B" key as a toggle on your computer to turn the screen black temporarily. A second tap on the "B" key will return to the last image on the screen as you continue.

Finally, sometimes the best visual is no visual, just you as the speaker making a critical point. You can insert a "black" slide in your deck that allows you to step to the center of the room or in front of the screen, make your point and interact with the audience, and then continue with the next slide at the appropriate point.

In summary, applying the five principles—concentration, clarity, consistency, correctness, and control—will give you the simple, professional visual support that decision makers like.

Remember, the focus should be on you and your ideas, not your slides. Your slides and other visual media simply support and reinforce your message. Your purpose is to deliver a clear, concise, and persuasive summary of your idea, proposal, or recommendation in a way that connects with and meets the needs of your audience.

The decision makers in the audience will be making a gut judgment about you as you speak. Have you done your homework? Do you know your stuff? Can you be trusted to follow through on details? Effective design and use of your visuals, applying the "Five C's," will contribute positively to their conclusion.

Designing the Handout

As a reminder, our discussion about persuasive business presentations assumes a conference room setting. Our premise for the presentation design is that we want to deliver a short oral presentation, about 10 but no more than 15 minutes in length, in the style of an executive summary. Our goal is to present clearly and concisely our key points and "big ideas." This synopsis sets the stage for discussion and audience involvement, one of the keys to persuasion. A key element in this approach is the supporting document, or handout, which you distribute *after* the presentation.

Although the document could be in traditional report format, I prefer a "flip-book," a spiral-bound document in horizontal format constructed with PowerPoint or other presentation media (Figure 5.6).[6] I call the document a flip-book because the format and binding makes it easy for the audience to flip to a particular page for discussion versus a bound or stapled document.

During my corporate years, I had the privilege of working with a number of major consulting firms on various projects. They all used flip-books as part of their presentation support, and I found the tool to be quite effective in facilitating discussion.

To be clear, I am not talking about merely printing and stapling together your presentation slides. Remember, your presentation slides are big, bold, and simple. Without your verbal commentary, they would not be very meaningful for reference after the meeting.

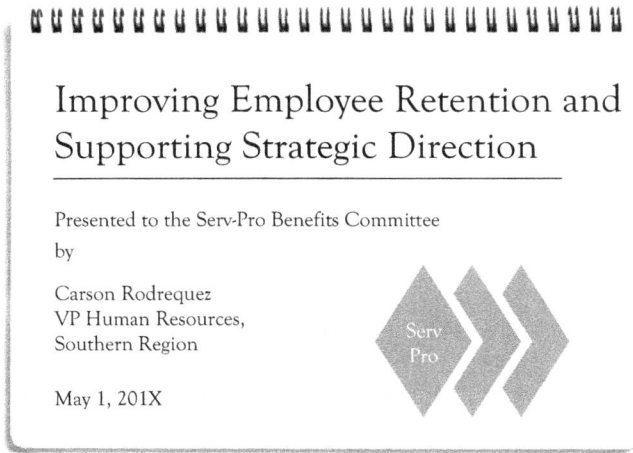

Figure 5.6. Flip-book example (cover page).

So yes, I am talking about extra work to build not only presentation slides, but also a more detailed handout. But, the extra effort pays benefits. A well-designed flip-book not only provides the text and background data to support your persuasive argument but also serves several additional purposes, such as:

- Promoting audience interaction and discussion
- Enhancing audience recall after the meeting
- Allowing people who did not attend the meeting access to your ideas
- Helping "brand" your image as a competent professional
- Providing backup if equipment fails

In the chapter on delivery and how to manage the Q&A session, we will discuss how to use the flip-book. In the context of this chapter on visual support, I will conclude by reviewing some guidelines for good flip-book design. Designing a report-style handout using presentation software is a different genre of writing and requires some different ways of thinking.

Because the flip-book will be used interactively in the Q&A section, the document needs to be easy to read and well organized. Like any report, an effective flip-book will include a table of contents, organized by sections, and labeled with page numbers. An executive summary section is also a good idea.

Design each page to communicate a clear point. Think of each page as consisting of three parts:

1. The headline states the main point of the slide. Compose the headline as if it were the topic sentence of a paragraph. In effect, the flip-book pages are a logical series of headlines that tell your audience a story.
2. Although the headline tells the story, the body of the page *explains* the story, using text, tables, examples, diagrams, and graphs.
3. The "So What" box at the bottom of the page summarizes the implications of the story in one short sentence; it is concise and to the point.

Figure 5.7 provides an example page from Carson's flip-book on the tuition reimbursement plan (TRP) presentation.

Referring to Figure 5.7, here are some checkpoints for the design of effective flip-book pages:[7]

✓ *Use a simple design, without background graphics or gradations, to avoid competition with your text and graphics.*

I prefer a plain white background with black text and a grayscale color scheme. Although the cover of the flip-book might be in

Employee turnover generates significant "hidden" costs.

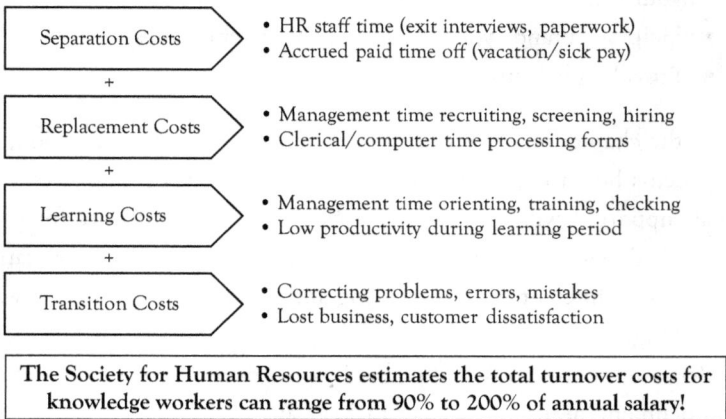

Separation Costs	• HR staff time (exit interviews, paperwork) • Accrued paid time off (vacation/sick pay)
+	
Replacement Costs	• Management time recruiting, screening, hiring • Clerical/computer time processing forms
+	
Learning Costs	• Management time orienting, training, checking • Low productivity during learning period
+	
Transition Costs	• Correcting problems, errors, mistakes • Lost business, customer dissatisfaction

> The Society for Human Resources estimates the total turnover costs for knowledge workers can range from 90% to 200% of annual salary!

Figure 5.7. Example flip-book page.

color, black and white is fine for the body of the report and in keeping with today's concern for cost economy. In addition, reports today often circulate electronically and print locally on black and white printers. The goal is clarity and readability.

✓ *Select a single legible font.*

Choose a basic, readable font such as Verdana or Calibri. You can use italic and bold for variations in style and points of emphasis. Be consistent in using left justification and sentence case.

✓ *Adapt the title box to accommodate a two-line headline, left justified.*

Set the font size to bold head, 24 points. This title box layout will allow you to use a newspaper-style headline for each slide.

✓ *Use the body of your page to explain the headline.*

For text, use font sizes 18 and 16. Avoid using bullets for all your text (boring!). Instead, place text in tables or shapes and arrange to show the relationship between ideas. Take advantage of the graphic features of the presentation software to build diagrams and charts to support your messages. Remember to leave some blank space on each page, allowing your audience to breathe visually. Avoid whole paragraphs of text.

✓ *At the base of the body, include an outlined text box the width of the page, containing font size bold 15.*

This section is sometimes called the "So what?" box. It is a place holder for a one-sentence summary of the implications of the content.

✓ *Include a footer at the bottom of the slide.*

The footer usually contains the copyright date, an abbreviated title, and a page number. Make the page number bold and prominent. The page numbers are how you guide your audience to a specific page during the discussion.

Note that the example flip-book page presents content that is too detailed for a presentation slide (remember Mayer's research). The corresponding slide used in the presentation might consist of a reinforcing image and text boxes with the words "Hidden Costs" along with the four category words "separation, replacement, learning, and transition" (Figure 5.8). As Carson reveals the category words progressively, he would orally provide

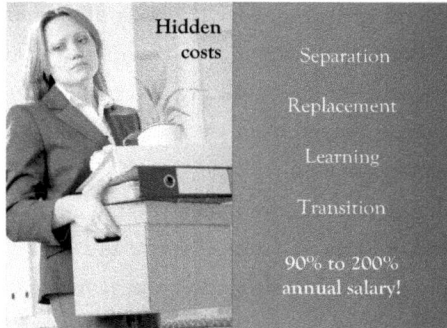

Figure 5.8. Example slide on cost of turnover.

examples of the four category costs. He could conclude by adding, using animation, the 90% to 200% cost of annual salary metric to drive home his point, referencing the source.

In summary, flip-book pages have a different purpose than slides—to help you navigate through the Q&A session, provide additional detail, and support post meeting discussion.

Table 5.1. Resources for Designing Effective Visual Support

Resource	Comments
Beyond Bullet Points: Using Microsoft PowerPoint to Create Presentations that Inform, Motivate, and Inspire by Cliff Atkinson	Shows how to engage audiences by combining classic storytelling with clean visuals; great discussion and application of Mayer's research principles.
Graphics and Visual Communication for Managers by Robert Sedlack, Jr., Barbara Shwom, and Karl Keller	Explains the fundamental principles of graphic and visual design for both print and oral presentations; clear, practical, and applied.
Guide to PowerPoint 2010 by Mary Munter and Dave Paradi	Provides excellent "how to" technical instructions for creating effective PowerPoint slides; useful guides on chart selection and design.
Slide:ology: The Art and Science of Creating Great Presentations by Nancy Duarte	Teaches how to think visually while modeling the principles of good design; beautiful and inspirational.
Why Most PowerPoint Presentations Suck and How You Can Make Them Better by Rick Altman	Delivers no-nonsense advice and provides many examples; the best source for instruction on proper use of the animation function.

Table 5.1 provides an annotated list of my favorite resources for those who would like to explore in more detail how to design bold and simple

slides and prepare flip-books using presentation software. Although some of these references are PowerPoint specific, the principles taught apply to all visual presentations.

In the next chapter, we will look at the processes for managing the logistical preparation, conducting rehearsals, and calming nerves.

Takeaways

Creating Visual Support

- People cannot read what is on the screen and listen to you at the same time. Use more images to reinforce your verbal points; reduce (or eliminate) the number of words on the screen.
- Make charts big, bold, and simple. Like highway billboards, the audience must be able to glean the message in a glance, and then turn to you for explanation and nuance.
- Apply the "Five C's"—concentration, clarity, consistency, correctness, and control. Each visual should
  - o represent one idea and concentrate on a specific point,
  - o be perfectly clear from the back of the room,
  - o be consistent in style and tone,
  - o be correct and error-free, and
  - o control delivery of information and focus attention.
- Use the animation function selectively to sequence and tell your story, but don't overdo.
- Do not use your slides for a handout. Design your handout in flip-book style to provide the details to back up your presentation and to facilitate the Q&A session.
- Remember, the presentation is about your ideas, not your slides. Your task is to engage the audience on a personal level, meeting their need for logic, emotional connection, and assurance of your credibility.

CHAPTER 6

Preparing for Delivery

We were in San Francisco on the top floor of our corporate headquarters in the boardroom, admiring the breathtaking view of the bridge and the bay. It was late afternoon. Our executive team was there to rehearse our division's annual business review presentation for the CEO and his direct reports early the next morning. We all felt somewhat intimidated by the surroundings—a deep plush carpet, a walnut conference table big enough to serve as an airplane runway, and a hushed silence in the hallways. The digital projector was state-of-the-art for the time, mounted in the ceiling, and focused on a giant wall-screen. However, when we hooked up our laptop and projected our PowerPoint deck, something was wrong—the colors didn't translate properly; greens turned a funny yellow, and reds looked muddy brown.

None of us being techies, we fussed with our laptop settings for a while to no avail; one of our team even took his shoes off and climbed on the massive table to punch a few buttons on the ceiling projector, but again without success. We asked one of the administrative assistants in the reception area to contact tech support, but everyone had gone home. We began to feel a little panicked. Finally, after much commotion, we were able to borrow a portable projector that worked with our laptop and some extra long extension cords from the training department. The cords on the table disturbed the ambiance, but at least we were able to complete the rehearsal and deliver a respectable presentation the next day.

The experience in San Francisco was another important lesson for me regarding the presentation process. I was part of the executive team and spent countless hours working with others on content design, developing visual support, and rehearsing for a flawless presentation. However, I was reminded once again that all that work could be for naught if you do not pay attention to the logistical details, which must be an integral part of the delivery preparation. I was the one who insisted that we arrange for rehearsal in the actual boardroom, but I did not think to schedule someone from the technical staff to be present to help us navigate the computer issues and other aspects of the environment such as lighting. So, this chapter will be devoted to reminding you of things you need to think about and do as you prepare for the presentation itself—checking logistics, conducting rehearsals, and managing your nerves.

Checking Logistics

Tips from the Experts:
Do preventive and contingent planning—then you'll always be able to present with confidence.

Claydyne Wilder
Point, Click, & Wow

By logistics, I mean co-ordinating all the complex elements, including people, facilities, and materials that must come together to support your presentation.

We take too much for granted. We tend to assume that computers will not crash, the PowerPoint version I have on my laptop will work on your laptop, and we will never forget our power cord. Based on my own experience, here is a checklist to help you avoid a crisis when the stakes are high.

✓ *Backup your presentation.*
   Create multiple backups. Port your presentation to a second laptop. Copy the file to a *universal serial bus* (USB) drive. Upload to the "cloud." E-mail the final presentation to yourself. Be sure that video and other files used in the presentation are in the same folder. Avoid, as much as possible, requiring an Internet connection as part of your presentation—it is just too uncertain. Use screenshots instead. Rehearse using each of the backup presentation files to make sure all the files work. Finally, print a hard copy of your slides.
✓ *Tune up your laptop.*
   Make sure virus and malware applications are up-to-date and your laptop battery will hold at least a 2-hour charge. Yes, sometimes, electrical outlets do not work. Buy an extra power cord and keep it in your computer case. Turn off the screensaver function, power-saving mode, automatic updates, and any other "pop-ups" that may disrupt your presentation.

✓ *Carry a portable digital projector.*

Even if your destination venue is providing a projector, as in my San Francisco experience, there may be technical issues. Today's portable projectors are small, lightweight, and powerful. Either carry one with you or arrange to have access to one at your destination. Double-check to make sure you have all the cables and cords in the case along with a spare projector bulb.

✓ *Replace the battery in your remote.*

The remote is an essential tool, especially if you are using slide animation, allowing you to seamlessly and unobtrusively advance to the next image without losing connection with your audience. You do not want to be fumbling with the remote in the middle of your presentation if the battery dies. Keep a couple of batteries in your computer case, and put in a fresh battery before any important presentation.

✓ *Become familiar with the room where you will present.*

If you are not familiar with the scheduled room, if possible, rehearse in the room the day before. Arrange for a person from the technical staff to meet you to help with projection issues and lighting controls. In some cases, you may be able to make some minor adjustments to the room layout to better support your presentation style, such as the positioning of the podium. If the room does not have a whiteboard, ask for a flip chart to be available.

✓ *Prepare an "emergency" presenter's kit.*

Carry a small bag with a variety of resources, such as fresh whiteboard markers, water-based flip chart markers, duct tape, painter's tape, a small screwdriver, an extension cord, a video graphics array (VGA) adaptor, and a three-prong plug. You will be surprised at how handy these resources can be in an emergency.

✓ *Seek to be the first on the meeting agenda.*

Presenting first is a big advantage. You can arrive early, make sure all the equipment is up and ready, visit with the audience members as they arrive, and present while everyone is fresh and alert. Use your "social capital" and persuasive skills on this one to persuade whoever controls the meeting agenda to give you this favor.

I am sure you can add to the preparation checklist from your own experience. Of course, even with all the preplanning, "Murphy's Law" can be in play. If the unexpected happens and you are not able to use your visuals, get out your markers, hand out the flip-books, use the whiteboard or flip chart, and engage with the audience. Remember, a major element of persuasion is trust and authenticity. The audience will be observing how you handle the crisis. Keeping a cool head and a positive attitude, perhaps with a dash of humor, will keep the audience on your side.

Now, with your logistics under control, let's discuss the rehearsal process.

Conducting Rehearsals

You may have heard of the TED conferences, where interesting speakers from all walks of life deliver short presentations on "ideas worth spreading." If you are not familiar with TED, I highly recommend you visit their website, click on the "Talks" section and the link "New to TED."[1] There you can sample some of the classic TED talks and observe how the speakers frame their stories, use visuals in a selective, creative manner to support their messages, and deliver in an authentic manner that engages the audience. According to Chris Anderson, the curator of TED, speakers begin their preparation six months (or more) in advance and within a month of the presentation are practicing the final version daily. Every speaker invests many hours in rehearsing the final product.[2]

> **Tips from the Experts:**
> It's just a matter of rehearsing enough times that the flow of words becomes second nature. Then you can focus on delivering the talk with meaning and authenticity. Don't worry—you'll get there.
>
> Chris Anderson
> *How to Give a Killer Presentation*

Although few of us will become TED speakers or require six months of preparation time, I share the anecdote to reinforce the key idea in this section: *practice, practice, practice*. We tend to spend so much time in the content creation that we shortchange our rehearsal time. If you are not well prepared for the actual delivery, you will be less confident. If you are not confident during your delivery, you will not be persuasive. If the presentation is important to your business and your career, it deserves the necessary investment of your time.

The key, in my experience, is to follow a structured and progressive rehearsal process. Following are the steps that have worked best for me. You can adapt them to fit your own learning style, but the time investment is not optional. The goal is to "road test" the material and get to the point where you can speak comfortably without word-for-word memorization and without notes, cued by your slides and other prompts in your presentation flow. You want to be free to connect with and engage your audience.

1. *Draft a script of your remarks*

   Some of the script writing occurs as you develop and frame your content. For example, in the opening, we identified a three-step process: gain attention, clarify your purpose, and provide an overview. Your oral remarks should require only a few well-crafted sentences under each of these steps. Read your remarks aloud to check for clarity and speak ability.

   Carson Rodrequez's opening for his tuition reimbursement presentation, which raised the issue of cost of turnover, is an example of how this works. If you recall from Chapter 5, Carson chose to use an image of an employee leaving through a revolving door. His script for his opening remarks to accompany the slide looked like this:

   Have you ever thought about what the revolving door of employee turnover is costing our company? (Pause.) I think you will be surprised when you hear the answer. My purpose today . . . .

   After your slides are close to final design, you can use the "notes pages function" in your presentation software to script your remarks under each slide. Remember to include transitions. Write for the ear, using shorter sentences and a conversational tone. When finished with your initial draft, print it in notes page view.

2. *Conduct an oral "talk-through" using the script (alone or with your team).*

   This step is analogous to stage actors reading the script aloud on stage in the early stages of rehearsal. Project your slides and read the scripted remarks. Test for clarity and flow. Make edits as necessary.

If you are presenting with others, the team needs to do this work together, providing feedback and helping each other. Keep repeating the process until you are comfortable with the content.

3. *Conduct an oral "talk-through" using the script before an audience.*

    Now it is time to refine your script and slides in front of a small audience. The idea is to have some fresh eyes on the slides and some fresh ears on the narration. The trick here is to get the right people in the room, experienced presenters with some knowledge of the topic and capable of giving constructive feedback.[3] In some cases, you may need to complete this step with your boss first, before you involve others. You will need to provide your audience with a background briefing drawn from your strategy analysis. At this stage, the focus continues to be on content, not delivery.

4. *Reduce your script to bullet points and key words.*

    Make the necessary edits to your slides and boil your narration down to short bullet points and key words in notes page view. Print for further use.

5. *Conduct stand-up rehearsals (alone or with your team).*

    Mimicking the presentation situation as much as possible, practice your talk with the bullet points as prompts. Each time, your narration will be a little different, which is good. Do not try to memorize word for word. With the slide as a cue, you want to communicate the main points without trying to remember the exact phrases. Practice the transitions also. Do everything you would do in front of the audience. This practice includes speaking at full volume and normal pace. Continue rehearsing until the flow of words becomes second nature. Then, you can concentrate on delivering the presentation with meaning and authenticity while focusing on the audience.

    Although I don't like to put too much emphasis on delivery mechanics (believing that passion, energy, and attention to your audience trump mechanics), the stand-up rehearsal is a good time to refine your delivery basics with regard to eye contact, body language, voice, and enthusiasm. Figure 6.1 provides checkpoints for behaviors you should consider. If any of these behaviors are an enduring problem for you, asking for help from a professional presentation coach may be appropriate. If you are well prepared and engaged

Behaviors	Basic checkpoints
Eye Contact	✓ Keep your eyes on the audience, not the slides ✓ Hold eye contact 3–4 seconds per person ✓ Engage people randomly across the audience
Body Language	✓ Avoid standing behind the podium ✓ Maintain good posture (e.g., no leaning on podium) ✓ Let your hands be free and work naturally
Voice	✓ Project your voice; speak to the back of the room ✓ Use a conversational tone, modulate, include pauses ✓ Minimize "verbal tics" (e.g., um, like, you know)
Enthusiasm	✓ Smile; appear happy to be there ✓ Project excitement about the topic ✓ Animate; communicate with your body

Figure 6.1. Checkpoints for delivery behaviors.

with your audience, most of these behavioral issues will take care of themselves.

It is a good idea at this stage, if you can, to video record yourself. You will see opportunities for additional refinement.

6. *Conduct a final stand-up rehearsal (with audience).*

This step is comparable to a dress rehearsal, again with your carefully selected audience from the original script rehearsal. At the conclusion of the rehearsal, ask the audience to help you brainstorm questions you might receive from your target audience.

7. *Create a one-page outline.*

Finally, reduce your bullet points to a one-page key-word outline. This outline is your "security blanket" that you can place on the podium or table for quick reference if necessary. A full-page version of my flow diagram for a persuasive presentation, filled in with key words, also provides a great at-a-glance reference in the context of the presentation flow (Figure 6.2).[4]

Please avoid carrying note cards or a holding a piece of paper with notes in your hand. These behaviors are distracting and suggest you do not know your material. Remember, you have done the research, you believe in your topic, and you know what you want to say. Concentrate now on making a connection with your audience, not your notes or your slides.

Presentation Planner
Persuasive pattern

Name   Topic

| | Gain attention | | Clarify purpose | | Provide overview |

Opening [ ] → Transition → [ ] → Transition → [ ]
→ Transition →

Body

| Problem: | Solution: | Benefits/concerns: |

[ ] → Transition → [ ] → Transition → [ ]
→ Transition →

Closing [ ] → Transition → [ ] → Transition → [ ]

Summarize   Call to action   Close with power

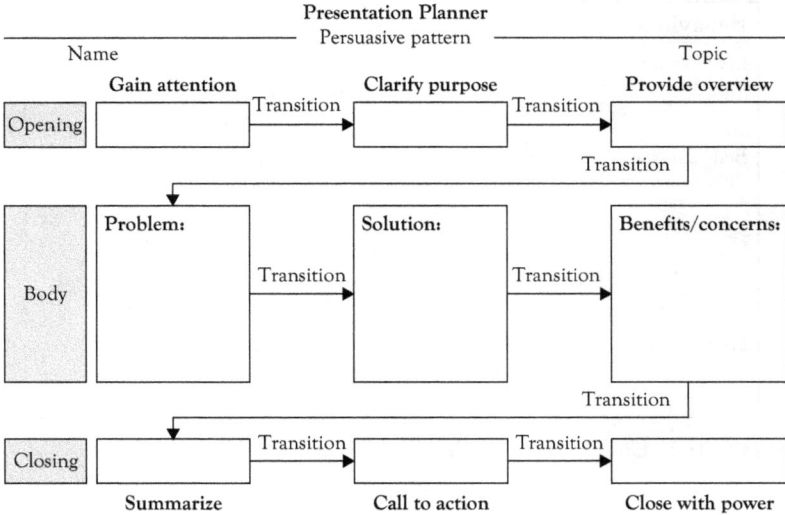

Figure 6.2. Add key words to the flow chart for quick reference.

I know these suggestions sound like overkill, but spending time in systematic and purposeful practice will make a huge difference in your confidence and the quality of your delivery. Relate the time you invest to the importance of the presentation to your company and your career.

Managing Nerves

> **Tips from the Experts:**
> Just before the talk, focus on the audience. Really look at them, their hair, eyes, chin, makeup—everything about them. If you do this with enough concentration, you will forget about being nervous, and you will have begun the all-important task of connecting with your audience.
> Nick Morgan
> *Give Your Speech, Change the World*

I have included the discussion on managing nerves in this chapter because the best thing you can do if you are nervous about your presentation is to prepare in the manner we just discussed, making sure the logistics are covered and rehearsing until you are confident with your material.

Feeling nervous is normal and necessary. You need the nervous energy to help you deliver your best effort. Part of the issue is psychological. Relabel your nervous feeling. Instead of saying, "I'm nervous," say, "My adrenaline is up." Adrenaline has a positive connotation, something necessary for peak performance. You can also use positive visualization. Run a little movie in your mind of you making a brilliant presentation and the audience responding with enthusiasm. Remember, the audience wants you to succeed. No one comes to a meeting hoping you will deliver a bad presentation.

To calm your nerves just before the presentation, here are some practical actions you can take.

The morning of the presentation:

- Use only the amount of caffeine you normally use.
- Avoid a heavy breakfast.
- Pump yourself up. Most professional speakers do some light exercise prior to speaking. I have found that even walking a few flights of stairs to get the heart rate up is very helpful.
- Do a quick walk-through of your opening and closing.
- Arrive early, recheck your equipment and materials, and then visit with the audience.

Just before the presentation:

- Consciously contract and then relax your muscles, starting with your feet and calves and working up to your shoulders, arms, and neck.
- Take several deep breaths from your diaphragm.
- Take a swallow of water to lubricate your vocal cords.

If speaking before others is truly a stressful issue for you, experience is the best anecdote. I strongly recommend participation in the Toastmasters organization.[5] There are a number of clear benefits. Meetings are local and usually held during the lunch hour or in the evening. You will regularly deliver short presentations to a live audience in a low-pressure environment, receiving constructive feedback. You will see many speakers (fellow members) perform, some good, some bad, and you can learn a lot from both. Best of all, you will quickly accumulate hours of practice and experience to boost your confidence.

With the preparation in place, we are ready to talk about the actual delivery of the presentation in our final chapter.

Takeaways

Preparing for Delivery

- Manage the logistics in advance by co-ordinating all the elements that must come together to support your presentation: These include the following:
  - Back up your presentation in multiple ways.
  - Tune up your laptop.
  - Arrange for a portable digital projector as backup.
  - Replace batteries.
  - Become familiar with the room where you will present.
  - Ensure technical support people are available.
  - Prepare an emergency presenter's kit.
  - Seek to be first on the agenda.
- Practice, practice, practice. Follow a structured rehearsal plan:
  - Draft a complete script of your remarks; include transitions and key to your slides.
  - Conduct an oral reading of the script in tandem with your slides, edit for clarity and flow, and tune for eyes and ears.
  - Conduct a second oral reading with a selected audience new to the material, again focusing on content and slide design, not delivery.
  - Reduce the script to short bullet points, key words, and symbols.
  - Conduct repeated stand-up oral rehearsals until the flow of words becomes second nature; then concentrate on using eye contact, body language, and voice to connect with the audience.
  - Conduct a final "dress" rehearsal with your selected audience.
  - Construct a one-page outline of key points or create a flow diagram of key words to have on the podium for reference.

- Be proactive about managing your nerves:
  - Accept nervousness as a good thing—a source of energy.
  - Change the input to your mind by describing your feelings with positive words, for example, adrenalin; visualize success.
  - Physically pump yourself up just before the presentation.
  - Mingle with and concentrate on the audience, not yourself.
  - Breathe deeply from the diaphragm just before you speak.

CHAPTER 7

Delivering the Presentation

This is the big day, the culmination of a lot of hard work. Now it is time to enjoy the benefit. Join me as we observe Carson Rodrequez presenting to the Serv-Pro corporate benefits committee in the executive conference room.

Preparation

The meeting is scheduled to start at 8:30 a.m. Carson arrived at 7:30 a.m. and has been busy double-checking his equipment and materials and conducting a quick walk-through of his opening. He has arranged though his boss to be first on the agenda.

Carson is neatly groomed and dressed smartly in a conservative suit and tie. He knows that that the dress code at headquarters tends to be "coats and jackets off" for meetings, so he wants to be one-step up as a presenter. He has removed his keys and loose change from his pocket and turned off his cell phone. The slide projector is on and the first slide is up, but the screen is black, reflecting the use of the "B" key on the laptop. Verifying seating protocols in advance, Carson has staked out a seat at the table with his notepad portfolio. A list of participants and their positions are on the table beneath his notepad.

Carson greets each member of the committee as he or she arrives. He has met some of the members before. With those he has not met, he tries to chat with each person for a few moments to learn a little about their responsibilities and interests.

> **Tips from the Experts:**
> Audience interest is directly proportionate to the presenter's preparation.
> Nancy Duarte
> *Resonate*

The chair of the committee, the Executive VP of Finance, calls the meeting to order promptly at 8:30 a.m. He reviews the meeting agenda and then asks Carson's boss, Susan, to frame the first topic and introduce Carson. While seated at the table, Susan summarizes her charge to Carson and provides a brief introduction of his background and accomplishments. While Susan is talking, Carson takes a few deep breaths to steady his nerves.

Delivery

Carson then steps to the podium, picks up the remote, turns to the audience, smiles, and thanks Susan for the introduction and the group for the opportunity to present his research and recommendations. He then moves smoothly into his opening, taking a step away from the podium and toward the audience, maintaining a comfortable, open stance. He gains attention with the image and question on his opening slide, provides a clear purpose statement with benefits, overviews his agenda and expected time required for delivery, and suggests the protocol for managing the flip-book handout and period of questions and discussion that will comprise the majority of his assigned time. He pauses to affirm that his game plan is acceptable to the group. You can feel the attention in the room shift to one of interest and anticipation and, perhaps, even a feeling of relief. This person clearly is an individual in command of his presentation who will not waste our time today!

> **Tips from the Experts:**
> End a sentence looking at someone, not at the screen. Linger a moment on the person's face. Don't dart your eyes away. Your audience will feel you are really communicating when you look at each person. Love your audience with your eyes.
>
> Claudyne Wilder
> *Point, Click, & Wow*

Carson then transitions into the body of his presentation, working systematically to build a case for the tuition reimbursement plan (TRP) idea by documenting the problem, exploring the possible solutions, and assessing the benefits and shortcomings of the options. He smoothly incorporates the elements of the Persuasion Triangle—logic, emotional appeal, and credibility—into his presentation. The story about Mary leaving the organization seems to strike an emotional chord with the group, as a number of the meeting participants knew Mary and what a great employee she was. Carson also enhances his credibility by responding effectively to a couple of interruptions by the Finance VP, who questioned some of the assumptions behind the financial analysis. Fortunately, Carson had reviewed all the data in advance with a senior member of the accounting staff who had signed off on his numbers. He uses that referral, along with some quick calculations on the whiteboard, to satisfy the VP.

In the closing, Carson continues to follow the persuasive pattern. He summarizes his main points, calls the audience to action with a specific timeline (asking for permission to pilot the TRP in the Southern region), and closes with power by linking back to his opening slide. He finishes the formal portion of his presentation in just under 15 minutes.

Throughout the presentation, Carson maintains good eye contact, speaks with enthusiasm, and lets his body animate naturally to reinforce his words.

Discussion (Q&A)

Carson then transitions into the Q&A by handing out the flip-books and takes his seat at the table to facilitate the discussion. He encourages participation by asking, "What questions or concerns do you have?"

As part of the meeting preparation, Carson worked hard to anticipate the committee's questions and need for details. He created flip-book pages to help him answer the anticipated questions and objections. For example, Carson asserted during the presentation that Serv-Pro's competitors were offering TRPs. A committee member wants to know more about what the

> **Tips from the Experts:**
> Treat questions as opportunities to give more detailed information than you had time to give in your presentation. Link your answers to the points you made in your presentation.
>
> Kitty Locker
> *Business and Administrative Communication*

competitors are offering. To answer, Carson directs the group to a specific page in the flip-book, which lists the competitors along with a summary of the features of each company's TRP plan. Carson is also able to provide some anecdotal information about the positive effect of the TRP on turnover in the competing firms, gleaned from some informal conversations with his HR counterparts during a recent conference. For most of the questions, Carson has flip-book pages to support his answer. It is clear to the audience that he has done his homework.

Throughout the discussion, Carson follows good Q&A protocol, which includes:

- Providing a three-step response. First, he rephrases or summarizes the question to make sure he understands the question correctly. Second, after directing the group to the appropriate flip-book page if applicable, he responds with a "headline" or short direct answer before discussing any details. Third, he verifies with the questioner that he provided a sufficient response.
- Breaking long, complex questions into parts. Carson uses his notepad to list the segments of a multipart question, then attempts to answer each segment separately, checking off the list as he finishes.
- Saying you don't know the answer when you don't. Carson maintains credibility by acknowledging when he can't answer a question and promises to follow up with the questioner and committee as soon as possible.
- Avoiding being defensive or submissive. When presented with a hostile question, Carson is careful not to become defensive. He attempts to reframe the question while acknowledging the other person's position. He works on creating a mutual understanding rather than trying to be "right."

As the end of the allotted agenda time approaches, Carson directs the committee to the last two pages of the flip-book, which reprise the content of his oral closing—a summary of the key points of the presentation and the requested action with timeline. He uses the pages to close the presentation, asking the committee again to take action and thanking the committee for their time and attention. The committee chair indicates that they will have a decision by next month. Carson receives enthusiastic applause from the committee members (a rarity) and several pats on the back as he exits the room.

After-Action Review

We don't learn from our experiences. We learn from *reflecting* on our experiences. Successful professionals always conduct an after-action review (AAR) for any significant event. An AAR is a structured debrief process for analyzing *what* happened, *why* it happened, and *how* it can be done better in the future. Therefore, within a few days of the presentation, Carson will spend some quiet time, perhaps with his boss, thinking about the answers to four questions:

1. What was planned?

2. What actually occurred (facts, not judgments)?

3. What went well and why?

4. What can be improved and how?

In addition, Carson will be sure to follow up the Q&A session by responding to the committee on questions he could not answer during the meeting. He will also send a handwritten note to the committee chair, thanking him again for the opportunity to be on the agenda.

To summarize our discussion of the persuasive presentation process, Figure 7.1 pulls together all the elements and criteria for an effective presentation. Use this worksheet as a checklist to guide the development of your persuasive presentation. The list can also serve as a rubric to evaluate your rehearsals.[1]

I would like to close by sharing a quote from Chris Anderson, the curator of TED talks:

Presentations rise or fall on the quality of the idea, the narrative, and the passion of the speaker. It's about substance, not speaking style or multimedia pyrotechnics.[2]

The problem–solution persuasive presentation pattern, together with the principles of the Persuasion Triangle, will help you focus your idea, shape

Problem–Solution Persuasive Presentation Checklist
Opening
✓ *Attention*: Gains audience attention with a startling statement, anecdote, question, or quotation; establishes common ground
✓ *Purpose and Benefits*: Provides a clear statement of purpose, describing the problem and questions to be answered; identifies benefits for the audience, answering "Why should I care? What's in it for me?"
✓ *Overview*: Provides an overview of topics to be covered; notes the expected length of the presentation; suggests plan for handling questions; asks for affirmation
Body
✓ *Organization*: Uses a problem–solution pattern; uses transitions and signposts to make the presentation easy to follow
✓ *Audience Centered*: Focuses on three or four major points tailored to the audience's interest and needs; uses appropriate language and examples; provides information needed to make a decision
✓ *Persuasion–Credibility*: Provides trustworthy citations, references, and/or testimonies
✓ *Persuasion–Logic*: Uses facts, evidence, data, and financial analysis to support the argument; interprets meaning and draws conclusions
✓ *Persuasion–Emotional Appeal*: Includes stories and anecdotes; uses appropriate psychological principles
Closing
✓ *Summary*: Recaps main points and reinforces the central idea
✓ *Call to Action*: Asks for specific, realistic action in a direct manner; provides the timeline
✓ *Conclusion*: Ends on a strong, memorable note
Visual Support
✓ *Concentration*: Focuses one idea per visual; titles tell the story for graphs and charts
✓ *Clarity*: Makes text easy to see—big, bold, and simple
✓ *Consistency*: Uses consistent fonts, upper/lowercase, and image styles
✓ *Correctness*: Avoids spelling errors, grammatical miscues, and math mistakes
✓ *Control*: Uses animation function to sequence and control delivery of information
Delivery
✓ *Appearance*: Dresses appropriately for the business occasion and company culture
✓ *Eye Contact*: Maintains good eye contact with the audience
✓ *Body Language*: Maintains good posture; lets hands be free to gesture naturally
✓ *Voice*: Projects voice; uses conversational tone with modulation; includes pauses; minimizes "verbal tics"
✓ *Enthusiasm*: Smiles; projects energy; animates body
Questions & Discussion Period
✓ *Preparation*: Brainstorms possible questions and objections and rehearses answers in advance
✓ *Handout*: Provides a flip-book or report at the end of the presentation that provides details and serves as a discussion tool and audience takeaway
✓ *Protocol*: Uses a three-part answer format—rephrase, headline, confirm
Bottom Line Impact
✓ *Does the presentation persuade me to take the requested action?*

Figure 7.1. Problem–solution persuasive presentation checklist.

your narrative, energize your passion, connect with your audience, and lead people to take action.

Use the ideas in this book to make a difference in your organization and your career. Thank you again for joining me in this learning experience.

Notes

Introduction

1. The literature reflects a variety of names for the tri-part persuasion concept. One common example is "rhetorical triangle." Based on my review of the literature, I believe the persuasion triangle model, as I have presented it, is original in design.
2. See Cialdini (2009) for a fascinating discussion of the six basic psychological principles that play a role in persuasion: reciprocation, commitment, social proof, liking, authority, and scarcity. We will examine some of these in later chapters.

Chapter 1

1. In addition to making notes on a long white board or using flipcharts, some managers like to work on their laptop and project to a screen through an LCD projector so that everyone on the team can follow along. I prefer the interactive nature of white boards or flipcharts. There is something about seeing all the information spread out at once and having the ability to work iteratively across the questions that promotes creativity and engagement.
2. For more information about the audience analysis factors and their application, see the following:
   • Demographics: Lucas (2007)
   • Decision Styles: Williams & Miller (2002)
   • Personality Type: Myers (1998)
   • Learning Styles: Morgan (2003)
3. Tieger & Barron-Tieger (2007) provide one example of the research on how jobs preferences tend to cluster by personality types. It makes sense. You don't expect to find many introverts in sales positions.
4. Lucas (2007) provides some excellent advice on constructing an effective questionnaire.
5. Locker (2006).
6. The discussion on physical setting is adapted from Lucas (2007).

Chapter 2

1. Adapted from Locker (2006).
2. Adapted from Morgan (2003).

3. Morgan (2003, p. 95), for example, advocates taking questions as they come up, calling the approach "continuous audience response." He argues the approach is more audience centered. Others, for example, Shwom and Snyder (2012), suggest taking questions at the conclusion of each topical section or during transitions between speakers when you have multiple presenters.

Chapter 3

1. Reported in Lucas (2007).
2. Why three parts? This principle goes all the way back to Aristotle. As humans, it just seems to fit the way we think. If you're involved in a church, have you noticed that the minister's sermon or homily usually has three points?
3. O'Keefe (2002); Conger (1998).
4. http://www.sashacorp.com/turnframe.html provides a good compilation of turnover cost studies.
5. Allen (2008).
6. Cappelli (2004), pp. 234.
7. Benson, Finegold, and Mohrman (2004), pp. 323.
8. Manchester (2008), pp.226.
9. White (2007).
10. See http://trends.collegboard.org/college-pricing. The data is presented on the basis of annual cost for 30 credit hours and includes tuition and fees ($8,655) and books and supplies ($1,200).
11. See, for example, Shaw, Duffy, Johnson, and Lockhart (2005).
12. Cialdini (2009).
13. The Benefits USA 2011/2012 survey. See http://www.compdatasurveys.com/benefits-usa/
14. Cialdini (2009).
15. Adapted from Cialdini (2009), Cialdini (2001), Cialdini (2013).
16. Cappelli (2004), p. 220.
17. Manchester (2008), p. 226.

Chapter 4

1. Locker and Kaczmarek (2001), p. 234.
2. BrainyQuote. See http://www.brainyquote.com/quotes/authors/j/jack_welch.html
3. Goldstein, Martin, and Cialdini (2008), p. 147.
4. Bahra (2012).
5. Wilder (2008), p. 30.

Chapter 5

1. The idea on why we talk to our slides came from Jennifer Hebblethwaite, presentation consultant for Graceworks, Inc.
2. Mayer (2006).
3. I want to acknowledge Dr. Thomas Hajduk, who at the time was Director of the Center for Business Communication at Carnegie Mellon University, for introducing me to Mayer's work and interpreting the research in the context of business presentations.
4. Baddeley (2001).
5. Mayer (2006), p. 5.
6. There are a number of terms in the marketplace to describe the spiral-bound handouts that I call "flip-books." One term is "report decks," used by Barbara Shwom and Lisa Snyder in their text *Business Communication: Polishing Your Professional Presence*. Barbara has taught the concept of report decks as a unique genre of writing for a number of years, and she is the source of many of the ideas presented in this section.
7. For a more detailed development of flip-book design, see the slideshare presentation prepared by Enargeia Consulting: http://www.slideshare.net/enargeia/design-powerful-powerpoint-documents-presentation?utm_source=slideshow03&utm_medium=ssemail&utm_campaign=share_slideshow_loggedout

Chapter 6

1. See http://www.ted.com/talks
2. Anderson (2013).
3. On a personal note, I often find it is helpful to pull together people from outside your company to form the rehearsal audience, perhaps business people from your civic organization or church. This provides a fresh perspective and can be a great networking event.
4. A template file for the presentation planner in PowerPoint format is available from the author: garymay@clayton.edu.
5. See http://www.toastmasters.org/

Chapter 7

1. A Word document file for the presentation checklist/rubric is available from the author: garymay@clayton.edu.
2. Anderson (2013), p. 125.

References

Allen, D. G. (2008). *Retaining talent: A guide to analyzing and managing employee turnover.* Alexandria, VA: Society for Human Resource Management Foundation.

Altman, R. (2012). *Why most PowerPoint presentations suck and how you can make them better* (3rd ed.). Pleasanton, CA: Harvest Books.

Anderson, C. (2013, June). How to give a killer presentation: Lessons from TED. *Harvard Business Review 91*, 121–125.

Atkinson, C. (2005). *Beyond bullet points: Using Microsoft PowerPoint to create presentations that inform, motivate, and inspire.* Redmond, WA: Microsoft Press.

Baddeley, A. D. (2001, November). Is working memory still working? *American Psychologist*, 851–864.

Bahra, P. (2012, December 27). The science behind persuading people. *The Wall Street Journal*, pp. D4.

Benson, G. S., Finegold, D., & Mohrman, S. A. (2004). You paid for the skills, now keep them: Tuition reimbursement and voluntary turnover. *Academy of Management Journal 47*, 315–331.

Bly, R. W. (2008). *Persuasive presentations for business.* New York, NY: Entrepreneur Press.

Cappelli, P. (2004). Why do employers pay for college? *Journal of Econometrics 121*, 213–241.

Cialdini, R. B. (2001, October). Harnessing the science of persuasion. *Harvard Business Review 79*, 72–79.

Cialdini, R. B. (2009). *Influence: Science and practice* (5th ed.). Boston, MA: Pearson Education.

Cialdini, R. B. (2013, July–August). The uses (and abuses) of influence: Interview with Robert Cialdini by Sarah Cliffe. *Harvard Business Review 91*, 76–81.

Conger, J. (1998, May–June). The necessary art of persuasion. *Harvard Business Review 76*, 84–95.

Duarte, N. (2008). *Slide:ology: The art and science of creating great presentations.* Sebastopol, CA: O'Reilly Media.

Duarte, N. (2010). *Resonate: Present visual stories that transform audiences.* Hoboken, NJ: John Wiley & Sons.

Goldstein, N. J., Martin, S. J., & Cialdini, R. B. (2008). *Yes! 50 scientifically proven ways to be persuasive.* New York, NY: Free Press.

Gordon, J. (2006). *Presentations that change minds: Strategies to persuade, convince, and get results.* New York, NY: McGraw-Hill.

Locker, K. O. (2006). *Business and administrative communication* (7th ed.). New York, NY: McGraw-Hill.

Locker, K. O., & Kaczmarek, S. K. (2001). *Business communication: Building critical skills.* New York, NY: McGraw-Hill.

Lucas, S. E. (2007). *The art of public speaking* (9th ed.). Boston, MA: McGraw-Hill.

Manchester, C. F. (2008). The effect of tuition reimbursement on turnover: A case study analysis. In S. Bender, J. Lane, K. Snow, F. Andersson, & T. von Wachter (Eds.), *The analysis of firms and employees: Quantitative and qualitative approaches* (pp. 197–228). Chicago, IL: University of Chicago Press

Mayer, R. E. (2006). *Multimedia learning.* New York, NY: Cambridge University Press.

Morgan, N. (2005). *Give your speech, change the world: How to move your audience to action.* Boston, MA: Harvard Business School Press.

Munter, M., & Paradi D. (2012). *Guide to PowerPoint 2010.* Upper Saddle River, NJ: Pearson Education.

Myers, I. B. (1998). *Introduction to type* (6th ed.). Palo Alto, CA: Consulting Psychologists Press.

O'Keefe, D. J. (2002). *Persuasion: Theory and research* (2nd ed.). Thousand Oaks, CA: Sage Publications.

Sedlack, R., Jr., Shwom, B., & Keller, K. (2008). *Graphics and visual communication for managers.* Managerial Communication Series, vol. 4, J. S. O'Rourke IV, series editor. Mason, OH: Thomson South-Western.

Shaw, J. D., Duffy, M. K., Johnson, J. L., & Lockhart, D. E. (2005). Turnover, social capital losses, and performance. *The Academy of Management Journal 48,* 594–606.

Shwom, B., & Snyder, L. (2012). Business communication: Polishing your professional presence. Upper Saddle River, NJ: Pearson Education.

Souter, N. (2007). *Persuasive presentations: How to get the response you need.* New York, NY: Ilex Press.

Tieger, P. B., & Barron-Tieger, B. (2007). *Do what you are: Discover the perfect career for you through the secrets of personality type.* Boston, MA: Little, Brown, and Co.

White, E. (2007, May 21). Corporate tuition aid appears to keep workers loyal. *The Wall Street Journal,* pp. B4.

Wilder, C. (2008). *Point, click, and wow: The techniques and habits of successful presenters* (3rd ed.). San Francisco, CA: Pfeiffer.

Williams, G. A., & Miller, R. B. (2002, May). Change the way you persuade. *Harvard Business Review 80,* 65–74.

Index

OTHER TITLES IN THE CORPORATE COMMUNICATION COLLECTION

Debbie DuFrene, Stephen F. Austin State University, Collection Editor

- *Managing Investor Relations: Strategies for Effective Communication* by Alexander Laskin
- *Managing Virtual Teams* by Debbie DuFrene and Carol Lehman
- *Corporate Communication: Tactical Guidelines for Strategic Practice* by Michael Goodman and Peter B. Hirsch
- *Communication Strategies for Today's Managerial Leader* by Deborah Roebuck
- *Communication in Responsible Business: Strategies, Concepts, and Cases* by Roger N. Conaway and Oliver Laasch
- *Web Content: A Writer's Guide* by Janet Mizrahi
- *Intercultural Communication for Managers* by Michael B. Goodman
- *Today's Business Communication: A How-To Guide for the Modern Professional* by Jason L. Snyder and Robert Forbus
- *Fundamentals of Writing for Marketing and Public Relations: A Step-by-Step Guide for Quick and Effective Results* by Janet Mizrahi
- *Managerial Communication: Evaluating the Right Dose* by Johnson J. David

FORTHCOMING TITLES IN THIS COLLECTION INCLUDE

- *Communicating to Lead and Motivate 2/15/2014* by William C. Sharbrough
- *Leadership Talk A Discourse Approach to Leader Emergence 7/15/2014* by Robyn C. Walker and Yolanta Aritz
- *Communication Beyond Boundaries 8/15/2014* by Payal Mehra
- *Speak Performance 3/1/2014* by Jim Walz, Ph.D

Announcing the Business Expert Press Digital Library

*Concise E-books Business Students Need
for Classroom and Research*

This book can also be purchased in an e-book collection by your library as
- a one-time purchase,
- that is owned forever,
- allows for simultaneous readers,
- has no restrictions on printing, and
- can be downloaded as PDFs from within the library community.

Our digital library collections are a great solution to beat the rising cost of textbooks. e-books can be loaded into their course management systems or onto student's e-book readers.

The **Business Expert Press** digital libraries are very affordable, with no obligation to buy in future years. For more information, please visit **www.businessexpertpress.com/librarians**. To set up a trial in the United States, please contact **Adam Chesler** at *adam.chesler@ businessexpertpress.com* for all other regions, contact **Nicole Lee** at *nicole.lee@igroupnet.com*.

www.ingramcontent.com/pod-product-compliance
Lightning Source LLC
Chambersburg PA
CBHW071500200326
41519CB00019B/5811